Contents

Route dedicate this book to the beloved

Robert Daley
(1954-2023)

A collier and a socialist.

Paul Laverty
Writer

This has been the toughest one to make together, or so it seems to me.

Over four years ago Ken, Rebecca and I discussed the notion of trying to make a third film in the northeast.

It might not seem so, after the film is made, but at the outset and at many points in between, it is always a much more fragile process than it appears from the outside. It is a gamble.

As ever, we met brilliant generous people along the way who gave us heart and inspiration.

The ex-mining villages are unique. On one of my first trips I had the good fortune to meet John Barron, a minister, outside his beautiful old church sitting at the top of the village looking out over the rolling hills. Later that day there was to be a funeral. A young mother had walked her child to primary school, gone back home, and then hung herself. This image, and imagining her last days, haunted me for an age, and did Ken too, once I told him the story.

I met an older woman who listed the names of other young women who had taken their own lives.

Wandering around many of these villages it was striking to talk to the older members of the community who were miners, or family of miners. One remarkable lady in her nineties was a nurse who had tended the wounded (one was her neighbour's father, who still to this day lived next to her) from the Easington mining disaster of 1951 in which 83 miners died. Listening to vibrant people like her, and others who were involved in the miners' strike in 1984, bore testimony to a powerful sense of community spirit, cohesion and political clarity which contrasted with the hopelessness of many in the present.

It became apparent that 'the past' should be a character in our film.

As I wandered these villages, talking to young and old, and noticed how the dereliction of the high streets was manifest, I wondered about the inner life and spirit of the older generation as compared to the tragic story of the young mum who took her life. How did community solidarity, as best illustrated by the soup kitchens during the miners' strike, disintegrate into isolation and despair?

Other questions came to mind as Ken and I met up. How did a once organised working class with a militant union end up in the world of Ricky, the main character of our film *Sorry We Missed You*, who had embraced the free-market narrative and considered himself to be master of his own destiny, despite being manacled to an app that measured every moment of his working life. How did Daniel Blake, in our other story, end up alone, bullied, and picked off by the systematic brutality of state bureaucracy which targeted our most vulnerable? Ricky's life, and Daniel Blake's life, did not happen by accident but by a series of political choices.

How could we make the past manifest itself in the present, in this story?

As we travelled around these communities it was obvious that the infrastructure was disintegrating; shops boarded-up, swimming pools, church halls, libraries, but what was even more apparent was the number of pubs that were lying empty or had been pulled down. All of this, as ever, reflected wider changes in the economy since the miners' strike in 1984.

What if we had an old pub as a character, the last one in the village, hanging on by its fingertips? The last public space standing, connected to the past, but contested territory in the present? It seemed to us The Old Oak had roots stretching back that might help us untangle many of the conflicts and contradictions of the present.

I found an old notebook with the scribble 'Tommy Joe

Ballantyne has lost faith'. Where this imaginary character popped up from I do not know, but I was very relieved to make his acquaintance. TJ demanded his place in *The Old Oak*. It begs the question why TJ has lost faith, and it suggests the even more important question of whether he can find hope again.

In one of the villages I saw an older Syrian man walk the streets. He was dressed in his traditional clothes, and it seemed almost surreal as he walked past youngsters on street corners in their tracksuits with big dogs. He seemed oblivious to everything around him, and it was hard not to imagine that the poor soul had been traumatised by the Syrian war.

We met wonderful Syrian families both in the northeast and in Scotland who shared their stories generously with us and offered encouragement.

Due to ultra-cheap housing in many of the ex-mining villages, often owned by landlords who bought the houses online at auction, many Syrian families and families from inside the UK but outside the northeast ended up in ex-mining villages.

We heard too, from activists in the communities, that local authorities from other parts of the country had done deals with landlords in the villages and had transferred some of their own tenants, many with deep-seated problems, to the northeast, without telling the corresponding local authority. We heard the first inkling of such brutal policies when we made *I, Daniel Blake* and this was the reason the character Katie ended up in Newcastle. More irresponsible local authorities are doing the same, dumping their problems elsewhere instead of creating a coherent plan to resolve them. Prisons too advertised cheap housing in the villages to inmates.

Little wonder many of those who live there felt hard done by and were convinced they were carrying an unfair share of the burden without adequate support. This is the febrile territory the far right continue to take advantage of to sow their poison. It would have been easy, and perhaps more melodramatic, to have had this as part of our story, but we felt that the challenge of creating the character Charlie was far richer and more revealing. How does Charlie, a decent man, part of the community, get worn down by circumstances and make those choices? It begs the bigger question of how hopelessness, unfairness, and lack of agency in our lives, play out in how we treat each other. How does it lead to fear and hatred?

How does one traumatised community react when it ends up, side by side, with another? What we choose to see is another question we were fascinated by. This is how the character Yara came to mind and helped us open up the story. You have to have the curiosity to look, to understand. We met some remarkable people in the communities who did that with the newly arrived Syrians, which once again raises the eternal question of hope; what is its source, and how do we nourish this fuel for change?

Hope is something we wrestled with from our first conversations about this story back in 2019. In fact, it is something we have been obsessed with from our very first collaborations way back in the early '90s. Which brings me to the 17th of June 2022, when we shot a scene in the stunning Durham Cathedral, a day that will stay with me for the rest of my life. It seemed fitting too, that this was Ken's 86th birthday.

This is not the usual fare for production notes, but since this is the last film we will do with Ken I want to say something for the record.

We have made films together in many parts of the world and have attended many festivals and meetings of every sort. I have seen Ken operate under the most severe pressure, from being ill in Nicaragua on our first film, to the last day of *The Old Oak* nearly 30 years later, trying to shoot a massive scene in between thunder showers as the clock ticked on. From children to government ministers, he has treated everyone with kindness, and a gentle humour. He has deep-seated political convictions and will take political opponents head on, but never once, even at his most exhausted, have I ever seen him treat anyone of whatever political, racial or religious background with anything other than the deepest respect; it is in his DNA, and a mighty example.

One last thing. Directing a film, even with the best support in the world, is a lonely place. It's worse than a writer facing the blank page. There comes a moment when you decide to dive in or not. The team awaits, and many eyes are upon you. Following COVID it would have been easy for Ken to have passed on *The Old Oak*, which was always going to be a mighty challenge. There were many months of work and travel even when the film was just a possibility. Casting took over six months graft, and that's before the prep and shooting of the film. On occasions as he got back to the hotel at 11pm I did fear this punishing schedule, that would challenge a youngster in their 30s, would be too much. I am convinced his political conviction got him through. It might make him smile if I quote Saint Augustine from over fifteen-hundred years ago who said that HOPE had two beautiful daughters. One, the anger at the way things are. Two, the courage to try and change them. This has been his working life. What a skinny frame to carry so much courage.

The Old Oak
Screenplay

1. TITLES AGAINST BLACK

Sounds of mounting frustration and anger; arguments from a crowd in the street. The hum of a bus with its engine running. We hear voices from the confrontation:

                    MAN 1 (GARRY)
          Where the fuck are they from?

                    FEMALE OFFICIAL
          Please don't swear sir.

                    GARRY
          Answer the question!

                    FEMALE OFFICIAL
          From Syria.

                    GARRY
          Syria! Bloody hell man…

                    WOMAN 1
          What's that got to do with us?

                    MAN 2
          More fucking Muslims!

                    FEMALE OFFICIAL
          Please mind your language sir…

WOMAN 2

Why didn't you tell us they were coming?
Don't turn away... I asked you a question.
Why didn't you tell us?

MALE OFFICIAL

Once we get the families settled we'll visit
every neighbour...

WOMAN 2

Afterwards!! What good's that?!

MALE OFFICIAL

Please... we're trying our best...

YOUTH

Dump them on us... fucking tossers!

WOMAN 2

How many more busloads, eh?

MAN 2

Same old crap... never tell us anything!

MALE OFFICIAL

Just give us a chance to explain...

LAURA

It's a fair point... [to official] we should have
been told... but let's calm down first and get
these families inside... they're exhausted...

The sound of a camera clicking. A series of stills appear.
Photographs are taken from inside the bus.

Two or three Syrian families, mixed ages, around 16 in total, are inside the bus parked on a typical terraced street. Outside local bystanders have gathered together around the bus; their anger is mostly directed at two council officials who do their best to calm the situation. A few have cans of beer. Others watch from their doorsteps.

Images of angry confrontations. Garry, mid-thirties, and one of his friends complain to an official. Aggressive faces at the windows. One lad shakes up his can of juice and sprays it onto the glass.

Terrified children clinging to mothers inside the bus. Anxious Syrian parents, and elders.

Two locals, T J Ballantyne, mid-fifties, and Laura, mid-thirties, try to calm the situation, and offer some protection to the two nervous officials.

ROCCO

Fuckin ragheids... shot ma mate in Iraq!

OLDER MAN

Take them to live in your street... see how you feel eh?

FEMALE OFFICIAL

Calm down everyone... you can see they're frightened.

WOMAN 3

We're frightened too!

ROCCO'S PAL

Council fuckers! Shitting on us again!

                          TJ
Easy lads... they're just doing a job... trying
their best.

                        ROCCO
'Just daeing a job'. How many times have we
heard that shite!

                        LAURA
Please everyone... look, they're exhausted, the
kids are terrified... not their fault.

                          TJ
Come on folks... let them out... there's
toddlers and old folks in there... please, time
to go home...

                    ROCCO'S PAL
This isn't your pub TJ, fuck off!

                        ROCCO
Get tae fuck man... back to yer ain country!

Still of Rocco's group being held back by TJ. Another picture
of Rocco's girlfriend pointing at the camera.

                      GIRLFRIEND
Look Rocco... she's taking your photo!

Rocco spots someone inside the bus with a camera. He moves
closer.

                        ROCCO
Ma fucking photo, withoot ma say so...
fuckin disgrace by the way!

TJ
Rocco, cool it man, you're terrifying the kids.

LIVE ACTION. BY BUS AND INTO FAMILY HOME.

Rocco viciously pounds the bus window, provoking others, including his girlfriend, to jeer and shout insults.

Inside a young woman, Yara, around 23 years of age, stops taking photographs as she picks up her bag.

An official inside the bus leads Yara, her mother, her two younger brothers, and young sister off the bus.

Rocco has his eye on her and follows her. As Yara moves off the bus towards the house, Rocco sneaks in and snatches the camera from her.

For a second he holds it up victoriously.

ROCCO
Yes!

YOUTH
That'll fucking teach you!

Yara throws down her bag and struggles to grab the camera back from him, cursing Rocco furiously in Arabic. She adds a few words in English too. Rocco is surprised by her fight-back and tries to hold her back.

YARA
Give me my camera!

ROCCO
Crazy bitch! Back off!

                    TJ
Rocco! That's enough!

                    ROCCO
[Invading her space] Come oan, one wee selfie
first!

In the confrontation the camera crashes to the ground.

                    ROCCO (CONT'D)
Now look what you did!

Yara picks it up quickly as TJ pushes Rocco away. She can see
it has been damaged; she's deeply upset.

2. INSIDE THE HOUSE

Yara, Nadia, her sister, 10 years old, their mother Fatima,
16-year-old Bashir, and 12-year-old Salim, led by the official,
enter the house which opens up straight into the sitting room,
with stairs to the bedrooms visible to the side. The official points
out the basics and indicates the bedrooms are upstairs.

Yara and Nadia climb the stairs to one of the bedrooms. Nadia
moves to the window and Yara joins her, holding her gently from
behind. Down below they watch as TJ and Laura still deal with
some of the more inebriated adults and a few teenagers. One of
the men is agitated and continues to shout angrily.

                    NADIA
[Arabic] I want to go back to the camp.

Yara, still deeply upset, examines her damaged camera.

3. BEACH

Marra, a friendly little mongrel, splashes about in the waves.

TJ is on the beach by the village. He throws a stick into the shallow water, as Marra scampers after it; mutual enjoyment. Simple pleasures with nobody else around.

4. VILLAGE STREETS

TJ, with Marra on a lead, walks through the main street of the dilapidated village with its usual mix of boarded-up shop fronts, a single mini-market with wired mesh, one remaining charity shop, and a betting shop.

A few older men huddle round the entrance to the betting shop smoking as TJ passes.

> TJ
>
> Any winners lads?

Their faces tell the story.

> MAN
> Fucking donkey... could run faster myself TJ.

Further along he passes Molly (wiry, a nervous energy, a grandmother approaching 50) who struggles to push up the metal shuttering to a hair and beauty salon.

TJ lends her a hand as he passes.

> TJ
> What you doing here Molly?

> MOLLY
> Thanks TJ... got a little cleaning job... just a
> few hours a week...

TJ

Good. How's Max?

MOLLY

Stuck to that bloody screen… wish you were
still taking the football… that would get him
out.

TJ

He was good… a tidy left foot. See you
Molly… I'll be back to get my nails done.

5. THE OLD OAK

TJ enters the pub through the side door and goes upstairs to his
flat. He has a bedroom, bathroom, and kitchen-living room.
He fills Marra's bowl with water, takes off his coat, and gets
ready for work.

OUTSIDE THE PUB: TJ emerges carrying a wooden pole.

The facade is seriously decrepit. Even the 'For Sale' sign is worn
and faded. The name, The Old Oak, is falling to pieces too. TJ
carries out the ritual of trying to push the 'K' of 'Oak' back
into place, upright, after having swung round the wrong way
on the nail.

Cursing quietly to himself he puts the K upright.

As he heads back inside the pub, the K swings down again.

6. THE OLD OAK PUB – BAR

The daily morning ritual; a relaxed silence between TJ and
Maggie as they work.

Maggie wipes down the bar.

TJ starts preparing the fire. He rolls up old newspapers, places them in the hearth.

Maggie begins wiping down the tables.

TJ builds up the kindling around them, and carefully places lumps of coal on top.

He lights the fire, and watches the flames from the newspaper take hold.

He kneels there for a moment, staring into the fire, day dreaming, as Maggie works her way round the tables.

> TJ
> I'll have to sort out that K one day, Maggie.

> MAGGIE
> Don't believe it TJ. You love it… [She
> continues to clean] We all need a wobbly K in
> our lives.

They continue with their work for a few moments.

> MAGGIE (CONT'D)
> Did you answer that letter from the bank?

TJ continues to stare into the fire, rearranging a few lumps of coal with the poker.

> TJ
> Next week Maggie, I promise.

She doesn't seem convinced, but bites her tongue. She goes back to wiping the last of the tables.

> MAGGIE
> You said that last week, TJ.

TJ
[Prodding the fire] Aye, aye...

7. TERRACED HOUSE

A man in his mid-fifties, Charlie, comes out of his home,
along with his daughter, pushing his wife Mary in a wheelchair
towards his daughter's car. Their house is tidy, well cared for,
with a few plant pots by the entrance. But the house next door
is a shambles; cigarette butts strewn around, along with several
empty cans around the doorstep.

Charlie has spotted something further along the street and his
mood changes; a young estate agent removing a 'For Sale' sign.

CHARLIE
[To daughter] Help your mam into the car
sweetheart...

He strides towards the young estate agent.

CHARLIE (CONT'D)
Have you sold that house?

AGENT
Commercially sensitive information sir.

CHARLIE
I'll give you sensitive... how about that stake
stuck up your bloody arse!

AGENT
Don't tell anyone, it was bought online, in an
auction... along with three others at the top of
the village.

CHARLIE

Four houses... not even a visit. Who the fuck
bought them?

AGENT

Some company in Cyprus... I don't know the
details.

CHARLIE

For how much?

AGENT

Eight grand each.

CHARLIE

For fuck's sake! I'm screwed! How can I ever
sell my house? Have you got a tenant? [Rising
anger] Have you done a background check?

AGENT

Sorry, not my department.

CHARLIE

Not my department! You rented out the house
next door to us to a fucking nutter! Rubbish
everywhere, banging the walls, threatened
my wife... told the police to fuck off! So I'm
warning you... another fruitcake on our street
and I'll be down to your office!

6. BAR (CONT'D)

Charlie joins a group at the bar. Another customer Garry (a vital
quality to him), a close friend of Vic, has also entered the pub.

Charlie is exasperated, incredulous, as his friends listen sympathetically as he sups his pint.

                    CHARLIE
          … online… at an auction… three other
          houses up near you Jaffa… our village… our
          streets…

                    VIC
          Bought by some speculating greedy bastard…
          then rent it out to some moron…

                    GARRY
          They were advertising houses for rent in our
          street in Durham prison… like shitting on us!

                    CHARLIE
          Know who bought the houses? Some
          company in Cyprus! Jesus Christ…

                    TJ
          Bloody disgrace Charlie.

The others sympathise as Charlie takes a long soothing sip of his pint and takes a breath.

                    CHARLIE
          Remember when Mary got ill… we were
          thinking of selling up and moving close to her
          sister?

                    TJ
          I remember that… tough time for you both.

CHARLIE

We weren't sure... hummed and hawed...
the house was worth over fifty grand then...
know what those wankers online bought the
houses for...? Eight grand!

VIC

For fuck's sake!

CHARLIE

We're totally screwed... Mary can't stand it
anymore with that prick next door, but we're
trapped. She's going to spend her last days
like this... [barely containing fury, genuinely
overcome] this is our life... our home...

TJ

They don't give a shit.

MAGGIE

Poor Mary... it's not right.

CHARLIE

What do I say to her? Even the police do
nothing... I feel fucking useless... [pause]
Sorry lads...

ARCHIE

It's okay mate... good to let off steam.

The door opens and Yara comes in. She pauses, unsure of herself.

YARA

[To the bar] Good morning.

GARRY
[To Vic] She's one of them from the bus.

VIC
Holy fuck… that'll be a pint of Guinness then.

GARRY
And a ham sandwich.

ARCHIE
Cut it out.

She moves towards TJ behind the bar.

YARA
Excuse me, my name is Yara. May I ask your name?

TJ
Tommy Joe Ballantyne.

YARA
Mr Ballantyne… I want to thank you for your kindness when we arrived. But I have a question… I am trying to find the man [holding up the camera] who broke my camera… I need him to pay for its repair.

More stunned silence from the punters for a few seconds. But Tommy is struck by her demand.

ARCHIE
That's the spirit lass.

VIC
Whoa… fat chance pet.

She continues to hold TJ's eye.

> TJ
>
> I don't know.

> YARA
>
> He wore a shirt with black and white stripes...

This causes some hilarity.

> GARRY
>
> That cuts it down to the last fifty thousand!

> YARA
>
> I saw you talking to him...

> TJ
>
> I'm not a policeman Miss.

> YARA
>
> If you do remember... please let me know.
> Thank you Mr Ballantyne.

She walks out.

> CHARLIE
>
> [Almost to himself] That's all I need.

> VIC
>
> What a brass neck!

> EDDY
>
> Thought they couldn't come into a pub with
> alcohol...

ERICA

As if she owned the place... what next?

GARRY

They get up to all sorts when no one's
looking... saw it when I was working out
there...

Tommy is disgusted.

TOMMY

Give us a break... out of order.

MAGGIE

Tell you what... that kid's got balls.

8. STREET OF TERRACED HOUSES

TJ takes Marra for a walk through the village.

He crosses paths with a youngster, Linda, around 14, who is as
tough as nails. But her eyes light up when she sees Marra and
she bends down to pet him.

LINDA

Marra... here pet...

TJ

Hiya Linda... should you not be at school?

LINDA

Don't you start TJ... and don't tell my gran.

TJ smiles. He's not the type to snitch.

Suddenly there is terrible barking.

                           TJ
Jesus Christ!

Two fierce dogs, with lads behind them, bound towards TJ and
Marra at speed. Linda skips off around the corner. TJ swoops
down and picks up the petrified Marra as the dogs bound towards
them.

A few yards from TJ the dogs are pulled up on long extendable
leashes TJ hadn't noticed.

The dogs bark furiously at Marra as TJ tries to calm down.

                        YOUTH
            [To dog, shouting] Fuck's sake Chopper, calm
            down you big bastard! [To TJ] It's all show
            mate… he's a big softie… honest man…

                           TJ
            Come on lads… you can't do that.

                    ANOTHER YOUTH
            All bark mate… wouldn't hurt a fly.

                           TJ
            Nearly gave me a heart-attack… got to be
            more careful boys.

                        YOUTH 2
            My apologies mate.

TJ turns a corner by the mini-market. He's stunned to see Yara
confront Rocco who has just left the shop holding a plastic bag
with two bottles of cheap cider.

                        YARA
            You broke my camera…

                           39

ROCCO

Whit are yi jibberin aboot... you drapped it!

YARA

I don't understand you.

ROCCO

Fuck off back to where yi came fae...

TJ

Good coming from you... how would you
like to be told to piss off back to Scotland?

ROCCO

You tryin' tae fuckin intimidate me? ... No
way man. [Walking away] Whit a day Ah've
had... unbelievable.

YARA

You do know him Mr Ballantyne.

TJ

Don't waste your time with him Yara... he
drinks every penny.

He spots her disappointment and the camera inside its leather
case around her shoulder. He's struck by her tenacity too.

TJ (CONT'D)

[Indicating the camera] Do you mind if I have
a look?

She hands over the camera to him. He opens it up and examines
it.

TJ (CONT'D)

If you have a moment, can you pop round to
the pub? I might be able to help.

YARA

Okay.

They walk towards the pub.

9. THE OLD OAK

TJ and Yara enter the bar, the pub isn't open yet, and the towels
are still on the pumps. Maggie is wiping the tables where the
regulars usually sit. Surprise on her face. TJ greets her but offers
no explanation. He grabs a key hanging behind the bar.

YARA

[To Maggie] Good morning.

TJ leads her to a door which he opens with the key into a
darkened room, with blinds down, which was once used as a
lounge and function room.

TJ

Sorry... it's a bit stale... I'll open the
windows... hasn't been used in over twenty
years.

He opens up the blinds and the light streams in. Chairs and
tables are stacked in random groups. There is a raised stage for
performers, and at the far end a door to a kitchen with a serving
hatch covered by a metal shutter.

TJ (CONT'D)

Seen better days... used to be packed full.

As each blind opens, the sunlight reveals framed black and white photos mostly relating to miners, their work, their families and the '84 strike.

Simply shot, but striking and elegant.

Photos of blackened faces in tunnels only a few feet high. Others in cages, men outside pit-heads. Even a pit pony. And, following a disaster [Easington 1951], bodies carried out on stretchers.

Yara steps to the next set revealed by the opening blind; huge crowd scenes, tens of thousands snaking their way up the packed narrow streets of Durham during the miners' gala.

Another section is dedicated to the strike, and several men being carried off by the police. Another, with a policeman's arm around a miner's neck. Yara is on them like a shot.

TJ rummages in the cupboard looking for something. He pulls out an old wooden box. He blows the dust off it.

> TJ (CONT'D)
> Let's see.

He lays it down on the table, opens the box and pulls out three different cameras.

> TJ (CONT'D)
> It's not the same… but could you use any of
> these?

She is amazed. One is very like her own and she picks it up, examines it and enjoys the feel of it. TJ sees her eyes light up.

> TJ (CONT'D)
> They belonged to my uncle… he took most of
> these photographs… he was a miner like my
> father, but he loved…

YARA

[Cutting him off] People... he loved people...
I can tell...

TJ

I suppose he did...

YARA

[Examining the cameras] These are better,
thank you for the thought... [indicating her
own] but this one...

She hesitates.

TJ

I know a second-hand camera shop in
Durham where he bought these... they might
be able to repair yours?

She is quiet for a second or two.

YARA

Thank you, but I have no money.

TJ

Maybe we could trade these in... my uncle...
[pause]... he'd love to see a youngster like you
get a chance.

She's touched.

YARA

Are you sure?

TJ

Yes.

She fidgets with the camera, as if finding it hard to hand over.

TJ (CONT'D)
I'll look after it... I promise.

YARA
Thank you.

TJ
Where did you learn such good English?

YARA
We fled to a camp... I volunteered to help
the foreign nurses... we were there for two
years... in the first months I learnt twenty
new words every day... then I borrowed every
book, every magazine... That camp changed
my life, the way I see things... every day you
can learn, make a difference, it's a choice.

Maggie puts her head round the door.

MAGGIE
TJ! Got to go... some of the lads are in.

TJ
Right Maggie, I'm coming.

Yara lays the camera on the table.

YARA
[Indicating the wall] Can I look at the
photographs if you don't mind?

TJ
[Nodding] If the dust doesn't kill you.

BAR: As TJ gets back behind the bar he can feel eyes upon him.

                    VIC
    What's going on TJ?

                    TJ
    Nothing much.

                    VIC
    We know she's in there.

                  CHARLIE
    This is the one place... away from worries...
    where we can relax and just be ourselves...

TJ can feel the pressure as they wait for an answer. His silence
annoys Vic.

                    VIC
    Maybe it was a little trip down memory lane?
    Giving her the old sob story about the poor
    miners eh?

Garry chuckles.

                  ARCHIE
    [Sharp] Watch your mouth Vic!

                    EDDY
    We just come in to enjoy our pint TJ.

                  GARRY
    We don't want ragheads in our boozer.

                  ARCHIE
    Speak for yourself! She's not doing you any
    harm.

                        VIC
Piss off Archie.

                      ARCHIE
Can tell your father was a scab. And Garry,
you're a disgrace.

                        VIC
Pathetic mate... always looking back... the
only regret my old man had was that he didn't
go back to work earlier...

                      ARCHIE
And still ended up on the scrapheap... you've
learnt nothing.

                      GARRY
Shut it you ol' fart.

                     CHARLIE
[Conciliatory] Cool it lads, that's all over... I
come here for peace and quiet... where's Jaffa?
Could do with the crossword...

THE LOUNGE: TJ has a glass of orange juice in his hand as he
enters the lounge. Yara has her back to him.

As he approaches she still studies the photographs. He hands her
the juice but keeps a respectful silence.

He studies the photos too; this section of wall is dedicated to
the women who ran the soup kitchens during the strike. Some
group photos, others just of faces. Cooking, serving, laughing.

There is a particular photo with an intense energy; a group of
women with banner. Yara peers in and reads the words written
on the banner.

YARA

[Struggling to decipher] 'If you eat together...

TJ

[Finishing off for her]... you stick together'.
That was my mother... she always said that.

YARA

We cooked together too... before we fled...
sleeping under the stairs in case we were
bombed... what is this?

She continues to stare at the image.

TJ

It was during the miners' strike... I'd just
started down the pit as a youngster... they
tried to starve us back to work... we ate
together every day... [pointing] That's my
mother... she's passed away... you know
Laura... that's her mother too...

Another, dramatic photo: a dozen young men in the foreground
being chased by several hundred police.

TJ (CONT'D)

You didn't want to get caught by them.

Yara moves to another; a real sense of people power, tens of
thousands marching.

TJ (CONT'D)

My father's favourite. [Pause] He used to
whisper 'Feel the power of the working
class... it's in our hands... if only we had the
confidence...' and then he'd shake his head...

Another photo; marching again, sense of celebration, some with fists in the air, and head held high.

                    YARA
          They look so strong...

                    TJ
          Marching back to work, after being out on
          strike for a year.

                    YARA
          They won?

                    TJ
          No... no... we lost. That's the bravado of the
          defeated... and the anger of the betrayed.

FADE.

10. OUTSIDE A HOUSE

Laura, mid-thirties, is a spirited and irreverent force of nature; her family and TJ's have been friends from way back. She carries a mattress from the back of TJ's beaten up old van, with TJ's help, towards a Syrian family who greet them warmly at the doorstep. The mother is there, with two young girls aged twelve and ten.

The mother says something in Arabic which the older sister translates.

                    SISTER 1
          Mum says thanks... that will stop us fighting
          as we share a bed. [Indicating her little sister]
          She keeps kicking me in the middle of the
          night...

> SISTER 2

No I don't...

> SISTER 1

Yes you do...

> SISTER 2

No I don't! Stop saying that!

TJ and Laura have to smile as they see the mum shake her head.

BACK IN THE VAN: TJ drives as Laura sits beside him.

> LAURA

Pull in there... I've got some baby clothes
for a young mum... dampness up the wall...
child's got a cough already.

ANOTHER HOUSE: Laura jumps out of the car with the baby
stuff. She knocks on the door. At the next house the front door
opens, and an older man stands on his steps. TJ has the window
open and witnesses everything.

> OLDER MAN

Hey you lot... something you never get.
Charity begins at home.

She ignores him as a young Syrian mother Aisha, with a toddler
in her arms answers the door. Her face lightens up.

> LAURA

Hello Aisha... [to child] Hello Jamal, how's
that cough sweetheart...

They exchange a few friendly words as Laura hands over the
clothes, and Aisha thanks her.

BACK IN THE VAN, DRIVING ALONG.

> LAURA (CONT'D)
> Aisha's a great lass… but the baby cries… the neighbour bangs the wall and curses… stresses them all out…

> TJ
> You want to hear what some of them say in the pub after a drink… and then they spout off on Facebook… feeding off each other.

> LAURA
> What do you say to them?

> TJ
> What can I say?

> LAURA
> I don't know… that's why I'm asking you.

> TJ
> I keep my mouth shut… that's what I do.

TJ catches her looking at him.

> LAURA
> That's not the man I used to know.

OUTSIDE IN A BACK LANE.

TJ, Laura, and members of the family take in the bits and pieces through the back gate.

Some local kids sit around watching the show, including a skinny, withdrawn 12-year-old, Ryan.

After they bring in a bit of carpet and bag of clothes in a clear plastic bag, Laura hands over a second-hand bike to a delighted teenager. He is over the moon, and Laura gets a kick out of it too. Laughter between them all.

TJ, by the van, notices Ryan stare at the bike.

> RYAN
> [To TJ] Who bought all that?

> TJ
> Donations from folks who want to help… all second hand, Ryan.

> RYAN
> They get everything man.

> TJ
> They lost everything.

> RYAN
> We don't count, do we?

The Syrian mother comes out of the house with a plate of sweet pastries she has made. Laura and TJ take one.

> TJ
> Thanks.

She offers one to Ryan. He just stares at the strange looking cakes.

BACK IN THE VAN: They drive on. Silence for a few moments. Laura looks exhausted.

TJ (CONT'D)
Maybe you should do something for the local
kids too?

Her frustration explodes.

LAURA
Yes TJ, great idea!!! You take the football
again! How about that? [She can see he has no
intention] I never stop! Got my own kids, my
mother's sick, work, my husband complains he
hardly sees me... there's only a few of us and
some from the churches. You do something!
Fuck sake... what's happened to you?! You
used to be the dynamo... gave us all a good
kick up the arse when we needed it! And now
I've got to beg you to give me the odd lift in
the van!

TJ doesn't say anything. Laura feels guilty as she looks at him.

LAURA (CONT'D)
What's going on with you?

He still doesn't say anything and he can feel her eyes upon him.

LAURA (CONT'D)
TJ?

He just stares ahead, not engaging.

LAURA (CONT'D)
Are you okay?

TJ
Fine.

11. VILLAGE PARK

A relay race with youngsters, both Syrian and locals, and a few adults.

Rima, a Syrian energetic teenager, sprinting as fast as she can, now losing all her puff, hands over the makeshift baton (the inside cardboard of a paper towel) to the next runner and then nearly collapses into a bystander, short of breath and in a fit of laughter and excitement.

The race continues with encouragement from the others by the side, including Jamila and her sisters Mari and Alma.

Yara takes some photos with her mobile phone, including a few of 14-year-old Linda who is waiting her turn to run.

Laura, Joe, Archie, and a warm and positive local teacher, Brendan, and Vicar Margaret with a few of her fellow volunteers from the churches, have got the simple event together, along with Yara, Fatima, Bashir, Salim and Nadia, who have got the Syrians together.

Linda runs as best she can. But she is very slow and easily overtaken. She stops.

> VOICES
> Come on Linda!! Keep running! What's
> wrong with you?!

She drops down to the ground.

Yara and Rima run towards her. Laura comes with a bottle of water.

> LAURA
> Maybe you're a bit dehydrated darling... do
> you want some water?

Linda, who looks pale and faint, just shakes her head.

> LINDA
> I'm just a bit dizzy...

> YARA
> What have you eaten today?

> LINDA
> A bag of crisps.

Yara and Laura catch each other's eye.

> LINDA (CONT'D)
> I just want to go home and lie down.

> YARA
> [Arabic to Rima] I'll walk her home. Give
> Laura a hand with the youngsters...

12. STREET AND MOLLY'S HOME

Yara has Linda by the arm as she walks the unsteady teenager towards her home.

> LINDA
> Forgot my keys...

They head towards the door. Yara knocks.

Max, a taciturn, tough 15-year-old, opens the door and stares at them.

> MAX
> What do you want?

YARA

Your sister's not feeling well… is it okay if I
help her in?

He stares at her for a moment and then steps back to let them in.

Yara helps her into the sitting room and lays her down on a
beaten up old couch.

Yara tries not to stare but she is struck by the state of the place.
Bare floorboards, no curtains, and the most basic furniture.

Max sits down on a cushion in front of a TV and continues with
his video game, ignoring them both.

Yara props up a cushion behind her head, and holds her hand.
Linda lies back and closes her eyes.

YARA (CONT'D)

I've got a banana in my bag… could you try
and eat that?

LINDA

I want something sweet… that usually helps.

Yara looks around her. Max is still concentrating on the video
game which is far too loud.

YARA

[To Max] Do you have a biscuit for your
sister?

Max shrugs but doesn't look up from the game.

YARA (CONT'D)

Can I have a look and see if I can find
something?

MAX

[Shrugs] Please yourself.

He still doesn't look up. It's in Yara's nature to spot the details... as if she had her camera with her; a broken lamp and another threadbare seat. A litre bottle of Coke with an inch of cola at the bottom, and empty jumbo packet of crisps. She moves to the adjoining kitchen.

She opens one cupboard after the other; very little there apart from a few tins of spaghetti hoops.

YARA

[Calling] Is it okay if I look in the fridge?

Still no response from Max stuck on his game.

She opens the fridge door and again she is shocked to find so little. There are a few slices of cold pizza and half-empty plastic bottles of sauce, and a near-empty plastic container of margarine.

MOLLY

[Shouting] Who the fuck are you?

Yara jumps in shock as Molly, the grandmother, confronts her. She is livid and gives no space for Yara to explain herself as she bawls over her.

MOLLY (CONT'D)

Do I go into your home? Into your fucking fridge?

YARA

I'm really sorry... I was trying...

MOLLY

Get the fuck out of my house!!! Nobody
creeps about my kitchen!

YARA

Linda was…

MOLLY

Get out of my house! Keep your big foreign
nose out of my business… fuck off and get
out!!!

Grabbing her by the arm and pushing her out.

LINDA

Grannie… will you listen!

MOLLY

You shut up!! I'll talk to you later!!

YARA

I'm sorry… you don't understand…

MOLLY

My bloody home!! My kitchen! Get the fuck
out of here and never come back!! Fuck off!!!
Out!!!

Yara is hounded out and has the front door slammed behind her.

She is humiliated, upset, and at a loss of what to do. A neighbour
who has heard the commotion stares at her coldly from her
window.

Yara can still hear hysterical shouting from inside the house as
Molly continues her furious rampage.

MOLLY (CONT'D)

What the fuck are you doing letting a stranger
in...

LINDA

Grannie...

MOLLY

Pair of fucking idiots!! Her nose in the
fridge!!!

Yara walks off, visibly upset.

FADE.

13. VILLAGE STREETS AND YARA'S HOUSE, EVENING

TJ walks along a street, he has a bag in his hand.

He approaches Yara's house and knocks on the door.

Yara, with Nadia behind her, opens the door.

YARA

Mr Ballantyne...

TJ takes the camera out the bag, still in its leather case, and
hands it to Yara.

YARA (CONT'D)

My camera!

TJ

We were in luck... he had the perfect lens.

Yara is deeply touched and examines it quickly.

Salim and Fatima are now at the door too. Fatima says something to Yara in Arabic.

YARA

My mother says you must come in. Please...
just five mins... just a tea... you have to...

TJ

My shoes are all muddy.

YARA

Take them off! Come in...

He has to smile. He enters, closes the door behind him, and slips off his shoes.

Fatima brings in traditional tea with Syrian sweets and lays them down at the table where they all sit. Fatima says something in Arabic, nodding at Yara, and Salim translates. Nadia starts to laugh as she points at TJ's big toe poking through his sock. Fatima tells Nadia to mind her manners. TJ wiggles his big toe making Nadia laugh more.

SALIM

My mother says you have no idea what you
started... Yara will now photograph and speak
to everyone in the village. Just like the camp!

TJ notices how she holds the camera to her. It gives him great satisfaction.

TJ

How is it?

YARA

Perfect. Like new. [Pause] Shukran... do you
know what that means?

TJ shakes his head.

YARA (CONT'D)
Thank you... it goes with your name...
Shukran Mr Ballantyne... [pause] some words
flow like honey...

TJ is touched and, slightly embarrassed, he nods back.

TJ
Shukran.

Fatima offers him a sweet.

TJ (CONT'D)
Shukran... [tapping his stomach] delicious...
how's school Nadia?

She gives the thumbs up.

TJ (CONT'D)
And you boys... have you got an English
football team yet?

SALIM
I like the Sunderland strip... [indicating
Bashir] he's for Newcastle...

TJ
That's more like it! And how's the school?

SALIM
Fine.

TJ notices Salim glance at Bashir.

                                TJ
            [To Bashir] And for you... how's it going?

Bashir shrugs and carries off an empty plate to escape further
questions.

TJ is intrigued by Nadia's simple dolls.

                          TJ (CONT'D)
            Have they got names Nadia?

                              NADIA
            [She lists five names] These are my best
            friends from back home... I don't know where
            they are.

TJ is stuck for words.

Nadia jumps up and brings over a photograph from a piece of
furniture. She hands it to TJ.

                        NADIA (CONT'D)
            This is my Papi. [TJ examines the man, with
            a fine suit and open smile] Do you think he'll
            be able to find us here?

TJ hesitates for a second as he glances around him.

                                TJ
            I hope so pet.

A moment of awkward silence.

                             FATIMA
            [In Arabic to Salim and Nadia] Right you
            two... homework. [In English with a strong
            accent] Excuse me Mr Ballantyne...

They head to their rooms, leaving Yara and TJ by themselves.

TJ looks at the photo in his hand again and then up at Yara.

> YARA
> He's a tailor... quick hands, quick mind.
> His only crime was to look for his brother...
> [pause] He was picked up by the Shabiha...
> it means 'ghost'... state sponsored militias of
> the Syrian regime... my mother thinks he is
> dead... I know he is still alive.

Her directness and certainty knocks him.

> TJ
> He gave you the camera, didn't he?

She appreciates his sensibility. She nods.

> YARA
> I told him as a little girl I'd be a photographer
> one day... and travel the world. He's the only
> one who believed me... this camera saved my
> life.

She savours it in her hand, as she hesitates for a moment.

> TJ
> How's that Yara?

> YARA
> I have seen many things I wish I hadn't... I
> don't have the words...

A moment of silence.

YARA (CONT'D)
With this camera I choose how I live... and I
feel my father is with me.

TJ is touched by her character.

14. THE VILLAGE PARK

The school bus has parked to allow secondary students to get off
after their school day. (The village has no schools.)

Bashir walks through the park. Suddenly he is confronted by a
big lad Ronnie and his mate Jack.

Pandemonium as Max (seen earlier, Molly's grandson) records
Ronnie on his mobile; Ronnie assaults Bashir, who is much
smaller than him, pushing his head up against his, and then
head-butting him, cutting his brow.

Jack lands a few kicks too.

RONNIE
[Finger in his face] Now you gobshite, what
have you got to say for yourself?

He grabs him by the throat, swings him round till Bashir
collapses on the grass.

Ronnie, who is much stronger, kneels on top of him as a half-
dozen other kids shout in excitement.

Ronnie slaps his face, humiliating him.

RONNIE (CONT'D)
How do you like that?

Ronnie at last lets him up. Bashir is quiet and humiliated and
just wants to get away.

Ronnie continues to insult him, inches from his face, as they both walk along being videoed on the phone by Max.

15. YARA'S HOME AND OUTSIDE

Fatima cleans up a cut and nasty bruise on Bashir's brow.

Repetitive thudding sound from the front door that seems to go on for an age.

Bashir tenses up at every thud, his fury mounting.

> FATIMA
> [Gently, Arabic] Ignore him son... he'll go
> away... just trying to get a reaction...

OUTSIDE: Max, repetitively, kicks a ball up against their front door, from no more than five feet. Again, again and again.

A particularly loud thud. Bashir jumps to his feet and grabs a wooden broom by the door before Fatima can react and sprints to the door and pulls it open.

Max is stunned as Bashir attacks him with the broom, hitting him fiercely, several strong whacks that leave Max shaken, and then running, with Bashir screaming at him in fury as he continues to strike him.

BACK IN THE HOUSE – LATER.

Sombre atmosphere. From the stairs Fatima can see a glimpse of Bashir, through a semi-open door, sitting on the edge of the bed. He's trembling, disturbed, with his head in his hands.

Fatima approaches him gently, opening the door. It's as if he's in another world.

She sits on the edge of the bed and puts her arm around the trembling boy.

16. THE OLD OAK (SAME DAY – LATER)

At the bar; the video of the attack on Bashir is playing on Vic's iPad. TJ is behind the bar, while Vic, Garry, Charlie, Eddy, Erica, and Jaffa are on the other side.

> ### VIC
> Stop it there!! [Pointing to Ronnie] That's my nephew... listen to what he says. ('We know what you've done, you know what you've done') Can you see this Charlie? [Vic turns the screen round so that Charlie & TJ can see it] That foreign git was bullying girls during lunch... pushed one over... You can ask the parents.

TJ can't stand it any longer.

> ### TJ
> I know that boy... he's a quiet lad... I just don't believe that.

It goes down like a lead balloon.

> ### CHARLIE
> He attacked Max with a stick, could have lost an eye... do you believe that?

> ### VIC
> If you don't know the facts TJ...

> ### GARRY
> [Jumping in] Shut the fuck up!

> ### EDDY
> Cool it lads... we're just trying to figure out what happened...

70

Vic plays it again. TJ has gone very quiet, but keeps an eye on the images.

                    VIDEO/RONNIE
         ('We don't want bullies in our school')

                         VIC
         You see… something happened before.

                        EDDY
         Got you… he's responding.

                         VIC
         Young Ronnie's now getting threats on social
         media.

                       CHARLIE
         Bloody fanatics.

                        GARRY
         [To TJ] What the fuck do you make of that?

                        EDDY
         Cool it! [To TJ, placatory] Another pint TJ…
         Anyone else?

                        JAFFA
         I'll force one down Eddy [handing Eddy his
         glass].

                        ERICA
         I'm no racist… but I'm not happy about the
         school… all these extra kids… don't blame
         them… but some of them can hardly speak
         English… holds everyone back…

VIC

Exactly. Are there any more teachers?

JAFFA

Yeah, they brought in one who speaks Arabic.

GARRY

Great for our kids, eh?

VIC

Two in front of my cousin at the doctor the other day... trying to fill in a form that took up half an hour...

CHARLIE

Same with Mary at the health centre...

VIC

Funny they don't end up in Chelsea or Westminster.

CHARLIE

That's what gets me! Dump them on us! And the posh wankers tell us we're the racists! Makes my blood boil.

GARRY

What about the background checks... who are they married to? Who are their brothers or cousins?

EDDY

Everyone of them has a smart phone. Face to face with fighters in a war zone...

VIC

Takes only one to slip through... one crazy
Jihadi...

GARRY

Like that bastard who conned everyone after
some shitty little programme in prison...
stabbed two youngsters first chance he got!

EDDY

We just don't know... they turned up here on
a bus.

Eddy takes the two pints back to his table.

JAFFA

All these refugees, what they've been
through... to be honest, I feel sorry for the
poor bastards... 95% will be fine... Cheers
Eddy.

ERICA

But what can we do when we can't even look
after our own?

VIC

Dead on... people living in boarded-up homes
with fucking candles!

Charlie's frustration grows.

CHARLIE

We should draw a line in the sand... it starts
here... in this village, in The Old Oak. We
should organise a public meeting... get the
councillors along, the local press... everyone.

JAFFA

Need to be careful... it could bring in the
racists, there's plenty about... we don't want
that.

VIC

It's now or never.

ERICA

Where do we hold it? Everything's closed
down, the church hall, the miners' welfare,
even the school's gone.

Charlie turns to TJ.

CHARLIE

You opened up the backroom the other day,
maybe we could use that?

TJ

Been closed for years... covered in dust.

VIC

We could give you a hand to clean it up...
couldn't we lads?

VOICES

No problem...

TJ

It's a total mess... and the plumbing's falling
apart.

VIC

Jaffa's done time in the building trade...
Could you sort it Jaffa?

Jaffa looks uncomfortable.

> ERICA
>
> What about the cookers, TJ?

> TJ
>
> All jammed up.

> EDDY
>
> I'll strip them down for you... got time on my
> hands.

> TJ
>
> Health and safety Eddy.

> GARRY
>
> For one day! Give us a break.

> TJ
>
> Insurance... don't want you getting blown up.

TJ is aware of Charlie staring at him.

> CHARLIE
>
> A bit of a stickler for the rule book suddenly...
> [heading towards the lounge] Do you mind if
> I have a look?

The whole bar is now silent as Charlie heads to the door and
tries the handle, turning it aggressively. It is locked.

> GARRY
>
> [Indicating] There's the key... behind the bar.
> Open it up.

                    TJ
Closed I said.

                    CHARLIE
Some of us have been drinking in this pub for
nearly forty years, a lifetime. Me and Mary
had our engagement in that lounge... and you
gave a speech. We don't count, do we?

                    TJ
I'm sorry Charlie. It stays shut.

FADE.

17. STREET IN THE VILLAGE

Yara walks with Nadia, carrying the family shopping. Friendly
chat in Arabic between them.

Yara notices someone striding towards them on the other side
of the street and tenses up.

                    YARA
[Arabic] Run on home darling...

                    NADIA
What's wrong?

                    YARA
[Sharper] Go on! I'll catch you up.

Nadia runs off as Molly crosses the road towards her.

                    MOLLY
I need to talk to you...

Yara is unsure.

> MOLLY (CONT'D)
> I didn't know what happened with Linda that
> day... I'm sorry.

Molly pulls out her phone and shows Yara a photograph. There
is a striking photo of Linda.

> MOLLY (CONT'D)
> Linda showed me the photos you took of
> her...

> YARA
> I'm sorry I should have asked...

> MOLLY
> No pet... you don't understand... these are
> different... I showed them to the girls at the
> salon... they loved them... would you come
> round... take some photos of them too?

Yara is blown away.

> YARA
> I thought you were here about Max... hope
> he's okay?

> MOLLY
> A few bruises... he'll survive, he's a little shit
> sometimes... if someone was banging on my
> door like that, I'd give them a bloody smack
> too... [pause] Would you come to the salon?

YARA
Maybe I can take a photo of you too?

MOLLY
No chance pet... I'd break your camera!

18. HAIR AND BEAUTY SALON

There is mirth in the beauty salon as Tania the boss and her two assistants work with women of different generations, while in the background Molly is sweeping up.

Yara takes photos of them. (She is at ease and in her element with her repaired camera.)

Some get their hair styled, while others get their nails done. Young and old, an x-ray of the village. There is laughter, gossip and lots of chat, only part of which we hear.

Molly, very self conscious, doesn't want to be included in photos with those she would consider the prettier girls, but Yara catches a lovely one of her as she looks out the window, making signs to her grandson Max who doesn't want to come in.

As someone leaves the salon, Yara skips out too as she has noticed a couple of mothers with babies in their prams chatting in the street. She takes a few photos.

She crosses the street for a clearer view of the betting shop; a few punters puff away on their cigarettes as they examine their betting slips and commiserate. Yara captures the moment.

LATER: The salon is closed. Yara takes photos of the group. They then share a cup of tea as they speak to an older lady, Sadie.

SADIE
[To owner Tania] Do you do any gift vouchers?

TANIA

No Sadie... we're just a simple outfit...

Tania and the others spot her anxiousness.

TANIA (CONT'D)

What's wrong Sadie?

Sadie hesitates.

SADIE

You know my daughter, Josie... it's her
birthday coming up... she's hardly been out
of the house... it would do her wonders... get
her hair done... her nails are a mess... if I give
her the money... she'll spend it on the kids...

She takes out her purse.

SADIE (CONT'D)

If I gave you the money... could Josie come
here? Then she'd have to get out of the
house... know what I mean?

Sadie wells up. It gets the other women too.

TANIA

You're okay pet... [taking her arm] Of course
we can sort it out... haven't seen Josie for
ages...

SADIE

Breaks my heart...

ASSISTANT

I have a friend like that too Sadie... they kind
of hide, don't they?

This registers with Yara.

SADIE

That's it... there's no place to go anymore
with toddlers... they're so lonely...

She can't continue.

MOLLY

And feel ashamed... that's what happened to
my Katie.

Sadie takes Molly's arm for a moment; no words suffice.

SADIE

Have you got a little card or something? So
she can come round with it?

TANIA

Not really...

YARA

We'll make you one... my friend Aisha can
draw... what does Josie like?

SADIE

She loves her cat.

YARA

After she gets her hair done, I'll come round
and take a few photos...

SADIE

[Her face lights up] Would you pet?

19. THE OLD OAK

Before opening time. TJ changes a barrel, then wipes down the
bar as he listens to Yara and Laura.

LAURA

… it started off with the girls at the salon…
word of mouth… then to Sadie's daughter
Josie…

TJ

Haven't seen her for ages…

LAURA

That's the point… so many like her, hiding
away. Yara's been round half the houses in the
village…

YARA

It made me think Mr Ballantyne… our
families are isolated… worried for their kids…
some of the locals are struggling too…

TJ

You should hear the stories in here.

Another moment between Laura and Yara.

YARA

That photo in the backroom… your mother's
words… 'If you eat together… you stick
together.' Imagine the families mix… we eat
together… become friends… could change
our lives for ever…

TJ

Good idea, but a lot of work...

LAURA

Our mothers did five hundred meals a day
during the strike! We start off simple... the
families who need it most... Brendan at the
school knows the kids who are struggling...

TJ

You can borrow the van if you want.

Laura and Yara look at each other for a second.

LAURA

The church hall was the last space to close...
there's only one place we can do it... your
lounge, The Old Oak.

It's like a blow.

TJ

Are you trying to embarrass me Laura? It's
been closed for over twenty years.

LAURA

We can clean it up... get a gang in.

TJ

The electrics, the plumbing... for Christ's
sake!

YARA

Some of our men are builders... we could...

TJ

It's not safe Yara! [Fury at Laura] You should
have told her that!

LAURA

TJ…

TJ

Are you trying to ruin me?

LAURA

What?!

TJ

Even if I could open it… the regulars would
boycott me! I'm hanging by a thread as it is…
I can't sell the pub… haven't got a penny…
Do you want to see me on the streets? Get off
my back!

Both Yara and Laura are deeply shocked at the outburst.

In a mixture of fury and embarrassment TJ throws down the
dishcloth and walks off.

Laura is totally confounded by his blow-up.

YARA

I'm sorry.

20. GRAVEYARD AND WOODS BEYOND

TJ walks amongst the gravestones, with Marra running in and
out between them.

TJ reaches the grave of his parents, Frank and Myrtle Ballantyne.

TJ stands there for a few moments, quietly remembering them.

As he moves off, in the distance, there is the sound of wild barking. TJ looks around. No sign of Marra.

                              TJ
        Marra! Marra!

TJ runs from the graveyard to the woods nearby, calling as he goes.

Suddenly high pitched squealing of a dog in trouble.

Panic on TJ's face.

                        TJ (CONT'D)
        Marra!!!!

He starts sprinting among the trees; now horrific yelping.

                      MEN'S VOICES
        Get off you big bastard!!! Pull him back!
        Fuck!

More terrifying shrieks, then fading to a wail.

TJ can't quite orientate himself towards the traumatic sounds.

                              TJ
        Marra!!!! Marra… here lass!!!

He runs on, but suddenly there is silence.

                        TJ (CONT'D)
        Marra!!! Here lass!

In the far distance barest glimpses; he can see a number of figures run through the trees, and two big dogs bouncing above the undergrowth.

TJ is beside himself.

> TJ (CONT'D)
> Hey! You lot... come back, I can see you!!!

They disappear into the woods.

> TJ (CONT'D)
> Marra!!! Marra... come here pet!!! Marra!!

He runs around, desperately going back on himself, trying to figure out where the sounds were coming from.

> TJ (CONT'D)
> Ah fuck... Marra, Marra, come on lass!

He moves on, terror on his face. He pulls back some bushes.

> TJ (CONT'D)
> Ah Jesus... Marra.

We don't see the full horror. There is blood all over the ground, and half of Marra's lifeless body is under some bushes where it has been dragged.

TJ sinks to his knees and caresses his beloved Marra.

His face is grey and lifeless.

21. THE BEACH

TJ walks over the sand dunes cradling a bloody Marra; he has a shovel in one hand.

TJ finds a suitable spot and gently lays Marra's body down. He starts to dig.

From a distance we see him labour. He picks up Marra's body and tenderly lays it to rest. He notices the chain with the name tag round Marra's neck, and slips it off.

He covers over the body and lays a large stone on the spot.

22. TJ'S FLAT, EVENING

TJ sits in silence at his kitchen table.

His fingers twirl and untwirl the chain with the name tag. 'Marra'. There are blood stains on one sleeve of his shirt.

He hears the bell ring, but doesn't move.

He hears it again.

He walks down the stairs, and opens the side door.

He confronts Yara and her mother Fatima carrying bowls of pre-prepared food.

YARA
We were thinking of you... can we come in?

He stands to the side, lets them in, closes the door, and leads the way upstairs.

They walk along the corridor to the kitchen.

TJ watches as they lay the food out on the table.

Fatima whispers quietly to Yara.

Yara translates.

YARA (CONT'D)
My mother says... sometimes in life there are
no words. Only food.

It knocks him for six.

                              TJ
            [Quietly] I feel ashamed… after all you've
            been through…

Yara whispers the translation to Fatima.

Fatima quietly responds.

                            YARA
            There is never any shame in love. We
            understand loss.

Fatima indicates that TJ should take a seat at the table.

The women dish out the food before him. He is quietly overcome.
Yara and Fatima sit down opposite him. A few moments silence.

                       YARA (CONT'D)
            [Flicking her eyes at her mother] She'll stay
            here the whole night till you eat.

Fatima mimes with her hand, pointing to TJ, that he should
eat. TJ makes a start, as Yara and Fatima sit in silent solidarity.

FADE DOWN. FADE UP.

TJ and Yara sit opposite each other at the kitchen table. TJ
has finished eating and there is a half empty plate to the side.
Beyond, Fatima sits on an armchair within TJ's sitting room,
answering messages on her mobile phone.

Yara now holds the chain and name tag of Marra, examines it,
before handing it back to TJ.

                            YARA
            When did you get her?

                    TJ
        The 9th of April... two years ago.

                   YARA
     [Surprised] You remember the date.

A moment between them. TJ looks to his hands after a moment
and breathes deeply.

                    TJ
        I've never told this to anyone...

Another moment of silence. Yara's attention helps him continue.

               TJ (CONT'D)
        April, the 9th of April... a long, long time
        ago... my father died in a mining accident...
        a seam three miles out, under the sea...
        [Pause] April... 9th of April two years ago...
        I decided to take my own life... maybe that's
        hard for you to understand Yara?

                   YARA
        Maybe it's not.

Again she is quiet, letting him continue.

                    TJ
        I've made many mistakes... a divorce from a
        very good person I took for granted... I made
        time for everyone, but not her...

                   YARA
        Do you have any children?

TJ

I have one son. I don't see him much. He
blames me, for good reason. [Pause] Over
the years I began to rot from the inside out...
damaged everyone I loved... began to hate
everything around me... The Old Oak, falling
apart... the punters, bitter and burnt out, just
like me... their bile, pints for breakfast and
endless drivel... I wanted out, to start again,
but couldn't sell... I felt small, nasty, trapped...
sick of myself... my father was a brave
principled man... certain, generous, hopeful...
everything I wasn't... on his anniversary I
decided to end it all... but it's not so easy... I
had to find a trigger...

FLASHBACK TO THE BEACH.

TJ, rough and unkempt, walks along the abandoned beach.

TJ'S VOICEOVER

... so I walked to the beach... got my bearings
from the pit-head... and stood there on the
sand looking out to the horizon... three miles
out... if I could swim that far, just above where
my father died below... that would do me,
point of no return... I left a note on this table.
'Tommy Joe Ballantyne is going for a swim.'

TJ gets closer to the water.

TJ'S VOICEOVER (CONT'D)

I took my first step towards the swell... and
that's when it happened. [Pause] I'm not
a religious person... I don't believe in the
afterlife...

A little mongrel approaches TJ tentatively. TJ looks around but no one is in sight. The dog moves closer to him. Snuggles up to him. TJ bends down to examine the name tag.

> TJ VOICEOVER (CONT'D)
> … but this little dog appeared from
> nowhere… she was on her own… she came
> up close… looked up at me, snuggled into my
> foot… I saw the name tag… Marra. Marra!
> Straight to my heart… do you know what that
> means?

Back to TJ's kitchen. Yara listens intently as TJ fidgets with the name tag.

> YARA
> No.

> TJ
> It comes from the miners… an old word…
> it means 'equal, matchless, faithful friend'…
> your marra watches your back… keeps you
> safe.

Yara can feel her eyes fill as she looks up at TJ.

> TJ (CONT'D)
> Despite the name tag nobody claimed her…
> she gave me the strength to get out of bed in
> the morning… a lost dog gave me life.

TJ is embarrassed as he's overwhelmed. He lays the name tag down on the table before him.

23. THE OLD OAK, THE KITCHEN

A powerful hand scrubs away on years of grease and dirt on a solid industrial cooker that has seen better days.

TJ is in his vest, totally focused, cleans for all he's worth. Behind him on the wall are all the old discoloured ladles, spoons, pots and pans.

THE BAR: Laura and Yara walk in. Maggie is serving Jaffa, Erica and her female friend.

LAURA
[To Maggie] We just popped in to see how TJ
is...

MAGGIE
Good bloody question... [pointing to lounge]
Go on, have a look... and I've told him
exactly what I think!

Laura and Yara glance at each other and tentatively head through to the lounge.

They can hear noises inside the kitchen behind the metal shutter, which has been pulled down apart from nine inches above the serving area surface.

Laura gently pushes up the metal shutter.

TJ, face and arms all smudged, turns to look at them for a second.

LAURA
TJ... what are you up to?

TJ
What do you think? I blame you two.

The kitchen is cleaner already. They sense something new on TJ's face.

24. LOUNGE – ANOTHER DAY

Hive of activity; general view of the lounge from the kitchen. Two students roll out barrels from the lounge. Miscellaneous furniture is moved out by two of the Syrian men. The place has been cleaned up. Sense of a community coming back to life. TJ is in the middle of it all, with usual suspects; Yara, Rima, Fatima and another Syrian mother, Yusuf and Abdul, Joe, Jaffa, Archie, Laura, Margaret, Brendan the schoolteacher, and new faces Rosie and Finn, ex-miner and community stalwarts. There are also two students in their twenties and Betty, well known in the community.

There is a young apprentice electrician, Tony, nephew of Eddy, standing on a worktop checking an old fuse box on the wall in the kitchen assisted by Archie. TJ approaches him. Someone has also taken off several panels from a lowered ceiling which reveals an old water tank and pipes above the fuse box.

> TONY
> Replaced the fuses… the electrics need serious
> upgrade TJ, but at least they are safe.

> TJ
> Better than the shagging plumbing… hardly
> been used in the last twenty years… how's the
> football going Tony?

> TONY
> Got a game the morn… still knocking them
> in.

TJ
Good on you lad… best striker I ever had!

Tony smiles, clear there was good relation between them.

Two volunteers clean the windows.

TJ has a list in his hand as the team gather round.

TJ (CONT'D)
I've got a little list…

Guffaws of laughter. Finn smiles too.

LAURA
How many times did we hear that?!

FINN
And always as long as your bloody arm!

TJ
[Smiling] I have got a little list… Headlines…
solidarity not charity… we discuss everything
with Yara and our Syrian families… they
want to give. Safety! Tony is sorting out
the electrics and the shagging plumbing in
this lounge, make them secure… Jaffa, you
coordinate that with Yusuf and Abdul. Good
to see you Jaffa. Brendan, you know the local
kids and families who need the support…
we need the names and signed permission
of the parents… Funding… Margaret, we'll
depend on you as ever to contact the churches,
Archie, Joe… you do the trade unions and
the Durham miners… Finn, transport and
drivers for supplies, this man could organise

an invasion... [indicating the two youngsters]
Sarah and Michael... thanks for coming...
they're going to do some crowd funding and
social media... Laura, logistics...

JOE

We'll put that on your gravestone, 'Laura
Logistics'.

TJ

Who's cooking? Rosie?

FATIMA

We'll cook too.

LAURA

You should taste her cakes... to die for.

TJ

We'll need a rota, volunteers, shoppers, cooks,
cleaners... the whole shabang!

ARCHIE

That's a hell of a lot at short notice...

BETTY

What are you talking about man?

LAURA

[To Yara] Betty ran the soup kitchen during
the miners' strike... fed over five hundred
every day.

YARA

How did you manage?

                    BETTY
Very simple pet... you never take no for an
answer.

A smile between them.

LATER: Jaffa is talking to two Syrian men who are working
where the ceiling panels have been removed in the kitchen.
One is on a ladder working on the water pipes around the
tank, and the other is handing tools to his colleague. Jaffa is
below. Communication is not going well and Jaffa is becoming
increasingly frustrated and louder in his Geordie accent.

                    JAFFA
        [Frustration] Where's Yara?

He looks around for Yara, but she is deep in conversation with
Betty, translating for the Syrian mothers. Instead he tries a
language app on his mobile phone to translate key words for
him into Arabic.

                JAFFA (CONT'D)
        [Addressing his own phone] How do you say
        'water pressure' in Arabic.

                AUTOMATIC VOICE
        [In American accent] Can you repeat that
        please sir?

TJ is within earshot...

                    JAFFA
Water pressure.

                AUTOMATIC VOICE
Can you repeat that please sir?

JAFFA

Water pressure!

AUTOMATIC VOICE

I don't understand sir. Can you repeat in
English?

JAFFA

I am speaking English! And I want it
translated into Arabic... fucking simple!

AUTOMATIC VOICE

Can you speak more slowly sir?

TJ

Try speaking proper Jaffa.

JAFFA

[His best posh accent] Wateer Preeesure.

TJ

That's bloody Chinese... like the Queen...
[giving it a bash, into Jaffa's phone] 'One's
water pressure'.

AUTOMATIC VOICE

We have no words that match that
pronunciation.

JAFFA

[To the phone, up to his face] Listen in
there you deaf bastard... listen! WATER
PRESSURE.

AUTOMATIC VOICE

[Suddenly in Arabic, phonetic, sounding
roughly like] 'murton-miar'.

JAFFA

Bastard knew all along!!! [To the Syrians] The
pipes are dodgy, very old... and we've got to
check out the... [checking phone]... Ah fuck!
What was the word again?

TJ

I don't know.

JAFFA

You're fucking useless TJ.

25. THE OLD OAK, BAR

In the street, Fatima, and two Syrian women, each with a child,
head into the pub carrying various supplies.

Maggie, by herself, behind the bar, indicates they should leave
the supplies in the corner by the door to the lounge. They lay
out the boxes while talking to each other, lost in conversation.
Quite a noisy discussion between them. Then a couple of men
come in carrying even more stuff and dump it down taking up
even more space. Louder chat, and some laughter.

Charlie, Vic, Eddy and Micky, are really pissed off at the
nuisance and sense of losing their space; unacknowledged too.

The Syrians leave, saying goodbye to Maggie. They fail to close
the door. Vic gets up to shut it.

VIC

[Closing the door] For fuck's sake.

MICKY

We don't barge into their places, do we?

CHARLIE

Some peace and quiet man, that's all we ask.

The young apprentice electrician Tony enters from the door to the lounge, behind the bar.

EDDY

Tony... what you doing here?

TONY

Hey Uncle Ed... my boss sent me up to check the wiring.

VIC

Hope you're getting paid.

TONY

A favour for TJ, nothing to do with me. Got to rush...

EDDY

A pint next time!

Tony is passed at the front door by a man carrying a huge box of supplies.

He's followed by another two union members, one man and one woman, carrying even more.

SAMMY

[To Maggie] Is it okay if we leave these here?

Sammy notices the whole bar stare at him.

MAGGIE

Suppose so…

They lay them down, taking up more space near the bar.

SAMMY

Can you tell Laura that's from the Fire
Brigade Union… and there's more on the way.

Vic mutters his frustration under his breath.

SAMMY (CONT'D)

And can you tell her, Sammy, that's me…
found an industrial juicer… second hand
but in good nick, I'll bring it round later.
[Looking at them staring at him] Enjoy your
pints lads.

Sammy and the two union members walk out.

The faces of the punters are a picture.

VIC

An industrial juicer!

EDDY

What next?

VIC

A shagging jacuzzi!

MICKY

Fucking unions should mind their own
business… too much time on their hands.

VIC

Worse than the Panama Canal in here.

Vic gets up from his seat and moves to the bar.

                    VIC (CONT'D)
          Another pint please Maggie... anyone else?
          [No takers]

TJ and Yara come in to the pub carrying more supplies.

                    VIC (CONT'D)
          Bloody hell, how many more?

                    CHARLIE
          So the lounge is good enough for them... but
          not for us?

                    TJ
          Wasn't planned... short term, for anyone who
          needs a little support... all volunteers... your
          families too if you want... [Vic scoffs] Is that
          a problem?

                    VIC
          I'll tell you the problem... we drink in here
          every day, keep you in business, and you treat
          us like shit.

                    TJ
          That's not true...

                    VIC
          We asked you a favour, to hold one single
          meeting. One! All we got was a pile of
          excuses... but now with this lot you can't do
          enough. You're a two-faced tosser!

EDDY

Easy man...

CHARLIE

Cool it Vic... but it's like a bloody refugee
camp TJ... look at the mess.

TJ

Sad coming from someone like you Charlie...

VIC

You're fucking sad... can't make up my
mind... you're either looking for an OBE for
charity work, or you're giving her one behind
the barrels back there...

TJ

You better shut your mouth.

VIC

Fucking loser... even your own son won't
speak to you... no wonder your Mrs ran off!

TJ

[Rushing towards him] Fuck you!

TJ grabs Vic's jacket collar in a fury and holds him tight.

YARA

Mr Ballantyne!

It stops him in his tracks. But the loss of control delights Vic.

VIC

Ah... touched a nerve, eh [sarcasm] 'Mr
Ballantyne'. [Still face to face] Come outside
and we'll sort it out man to man...

CHARLIE

Leave it Vic, out of order! [TJ steps back] TJ...
this is the last public space in our lives, it's all
we have... we want our pub back... is that too
much to ask after all this time?

Charlie nods at Vic and Eddy who move to walk out with him.

CHARLIE (CONT'D)

You better make up your mind TJ.

Vic catches Yara's eye, who refuses to be intimidated.

VIC

And you, with the brass neck, nothing
personal... go back to where you came from.

YARA

[Firmly] If only you had a little imagination,
sir... that's what we want too.

26. KITCHEN AND LOUNGE, MEAL

Pure life; the lounge is packed with about 45 people, a mixture
of families, Syrians, locals, and the volunteers from the planning
meeting earlier. The kids are excited, mixed together.

The food is both local and Syrian.

Sadie, the mother of Josie, from the salon, is there with Josie and
her two kids who enjoy the company.

TJ, Laura and Aisha are dishing out food at the serving area to a queue of youngsters.

Yara has her camera and discreetly snaps a few shots. She notices Linda and Rima working together as they pour out juices for the smaller ones.

TJ's face looks different as he enjoys the banter with kids as he serves by the counter. Ryan and Linda are at the counter. Ryan has his eyes out on stalks at the amount of food TJ spoons onto his plate.

> RYAN
> All the grub… is that just today TJ?

> TJ
> A couple of days a week and a special on a
> Saturday night to cheer us all up.

He's incredulous.

> RYAN
> Can I come every Saturday?

> TJ
> If you want.

> RYAN
> Can I bring my gran? She's on her own.

TJ nods.

> RYAN (CONT'D)
> And we don't have to pay?

> TJ
> No Ryan… not a penny.

His face opens in a big grin.

LINDA
Is that a promise?

Laura glances at TJ.

TJ
We'll try our best.

Linda just stares at TJ for a moment. Then she walks off to a table.

LAURA
She trusts no one.

TJ watches her as she gets tucked in, eating her food too quickly. Two more line up for food. Rocco, still with his Newcastle top, and Angelina appear before TJ.

ROCCO
Hey, big man… thought I'd pop by and see how the newcomers are settling in…

TJ has to smile.

TJ
You've got some brass neck Rocco.

ANGELINA
We got sanctioned for a month TJ…

ROCCO
Fucking barbaric man…

ANGELINA

Only a few minutes late signing on...

ROCCO

Totally skint...

ANGELINA

I'm starving TJ...

TJ

Everybody's welcome here... everybody... [as
he serves out the food, joking] you can help
wash the dishes mind...

ROCCO

No bother... she's great at that.

Bashir approaches Yara and indicates she should follow him.
They go to the door leading to the yard.

BACKYARD.

Bashir nods at Max, standing up against the wall, and then
disappears very quickly.

Yara goes over to him.

YARA

What's up Max?

He is withdrawn; embarrassed. He shrugs.

YARA (CONT'D)

We've still got some food left.

Max tries not to react but his eyes give him away.

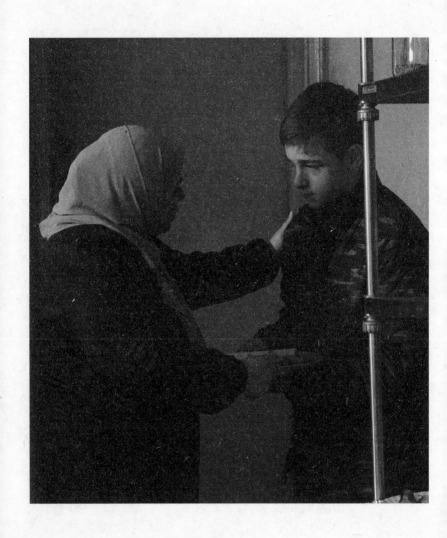

YARA (CONT'D)
What happens if you eat out of sight in
the kitchen... [he looks up] We won't say
anything if you don't. [Pause] Come on.

He follows Yara into the kitchen. One of the Syrian mums hands
him a juice in seconds.

INSIDE LOUNGE: Tommy steals a chip from one of the Syrian
lads as he walks past.

FINN
[To lad] Got to watch him!

A Syrian child laughs as a local kid copies him and sticks carrot
into hummus and then tries to figure out the taste; confusion,
but curiosity too.

TJ is at the back of the lounge, taking it all in. He enjoys the
moment.

27. YARA'S HOME, EVENING

Bashir is in his bedroom, his laptop propped up on his bed,
looking at a video message assembled by his sparky school friend
Karim.

These are miscellaneous clips, raw and unedited, with their own
rough soundtrack, interspersed with commentary from Karim
speaking into his own camera.

Image of Karim.

KARIM
Big news! You won't believe it... they built a
new swimming pool round the corner from
where you used to live... My sister Lina took

a video to prove it… all we need now is the
diving board.

Footage of some kids around a bombed out crater, full of dirty
brown water, now an ad hoc swimming pool. Half a dozen kids
are splashing around, still with their clothes on, having fun.

KARIM (CONT'D)
Now here is my little brother and his pals at
nursery school in the basement – not driving
me mad as usual.

Joyful clip of two teachers forming a circle with the toddlers and
singing a song as they skip around. Their fun is not diminished
by being in a basement.

KARIM (CONT'D)
My sister filmed this next one too… better if
Salim doesn't see it… but I wanted to show
you what happened to Osman's school, you
remember him?

Dramatic footage; the camera bounces around as Karim's sister
runs towards the school. Chaos, as bodies flee. A screaming
young girl runs past as the camera gets closer to the destruction;
an entire building of several stories has collapsed. Volunteers
scramble over the ruin.

A dazed child is carried out by a volunteer. Men scream for
a stretcher, and a bloodied adult is carried to a jeep. A young
female student weeps as she faces the destruction, horrified by
what has happened to her fellow students.

As the video is playing, Yara appears in the doorway, unnoticed
by Bashir. For a moment, she watches the horrifying images.
Then, quietly, she tells Bashir to come downstairs. His mother
has some news.

The pictures linger for a moment on screen, then Bashir turns them off. The screen is dark.

Yara and Bashir come downstairs into the living room and pause at the bottom of the stairs. Fatima is in the kitchen doorway, with her arm around Nadia, Salim at her side.

> FATIMA
> Spoke to Shadi... they paid a bribe to get their
> nephew out of prison... he saw your father
> two weeks ago... he's still alive... he's still
> alive...

Bashir goes to his mother, puts his arm around her. Yara joins them.

> FATIMA (CONT'D)
> Please God protect him... I beg you...

They huddle together.

28. THE OLD OAK: LOUNGE AND KITCHEN

Several volunteers tidy up as the stragglers finish off a meal. Lively warm atmosphere. Some Syrian and local kids sit together as they eat.

IN THE KITCHEN: Yara and TJ, in aprons, are cutting up vegetables for a big pot of soup for the next day.

TJ and Yara work away in silence, but TJ notices Yara is far from her usual self. More silence as they chop away.

> TJ
> Yara?

She shakes her head and continues to chop for a few seconds in silence, not looking up.

YARA

My father is still alive... someone saw him in
prison.

It shocks TJ and he stops chopping.

YARA (CONT'D)

Please don't stop... I can't say to anyone... I
sometimes wish he was dead, we had his body,
and I could bury him... [she continues to take
refuge in chopping]... A hundred to a cell,
so packed they take it in turns to sit down...
starved, beaten, few survive... that's what this
Assad regime does to us... it's the hope that
causes so much pain.

She can't continue.

TJ

I'm sorry...

She stops chopping and looks up at him.

YARA

I have to be strong for my family... for my
community... but it is all a big act.

TJ looks at her for a moment.

YARA (CONT'D)

Do you ever pray Mr Ballantyne?

TJ

[Shaking his head] All I believe in, is that
big pot of soup... and that we will share food
together.

A silent look between them, then back to the vegetables for a few moments.

A volunteer, with an ear to a phone approaches the kitchen.

> A VOLUNTEER
> TJ... a donation from the cathedral... Can you go pick it up?

He nods.

29. ROAD TO DURHAM

TJ drives. Yara is beside him in the passenger seat.

They turn a bend; suddenly they have a stunning view of Durham Cathedral in its majestic location, dominating the town and the countryside beyond.

> YARA
> Wao!!!

They approach a narrow bridge and TJ has to stop to allow two oncoming cars to pass. They have a good view of the cathedral.

> TJ
> Built by the Normans... nearly a thousand years ago. My father loved it... he used to say 'this cathedral doesn't belong to the Church. It belongs to the workers who built it. With all that ability and energy we have, why can't we build a New Jerusalem today.' [Pause] We never missed the Big March, the miners' gala.

> YARA
> Like the photos... can we go?

TJ is silent for a few moments.

> TJ
> You can go with Jaffa and Laura. [Pause,
> definite] It's not for me anymore.

Something about his face stops her from asking why.

30. THE CATHEDRAL

They have parked by a storeroom which is part of the cathedral outbuildings.

Geoff, a friendly volunteer, Yara and TJ are loading a substantial food donation into the back of TJ's van.

> TJ
> Thanks Geoff… this will keep us going for
> days.

> GEOFF
> We'll finish off here Yara [checking his watch]
> if you go now you might catch the choir.

Yara looks across at TJ, who encourages her. She leaves them at the van.

She walks across the precinct, a tiny figure compared to the cathedral's dominating presence.

INSIDE: Yara enters the main door at the west end of the cathedral. The voices of the choir reach her as she stares down the majestic nave towards the distant altar, and the stunning rose window above.

She walks down one of the side aisles, taking in the double row of enormous carved pillars.

She savours every detail and the almost unimaginable effort and imagination to bring it to fruition.

She heads towards the altar and carved benches for the choristers; she stands watching them, entranced by their singing, the young voices echoing in the gloom. It all touches something deep inside her.

TJ enters and spots Yara in the distance.

She moves on, her hand brushing a sculpted pillar. She looks up at the vaulted stone roof, and the light streaming through the stained-glass windows.

The sound, the light, the colours, and the sheer scale and beauty of the place begin to overwhelm her.

She spots TJ sitting near the entrance.

She moves down towards him as the choir concludes for the moment. Now a special silence. She takes a seat beside him.

TJ is aware that Yara is moved by the place. He knows it's time to listen.

YARA

> My children will never see the Temple in
> Palmyra... built by the Romans and destroyed
> by Islamic State... When you have half your
> country in rubble... and you see this... it
> makes me weep... What will my beloved
> Syria be like in a thousand years?

She wipes her eyes, and tries to control herself. TJ nods in silent solidarity.

YARA (CONT'D)

> [Looking up] How many years to cut the
> stone, lift the weights, imagine the light...

how many brilliant minds, how much sweat...
how many people working together... such
beauty... [almost breaking]... it makes me
want to hope again...

She can't contain herself and weeps quietly as TJ sits in quiet
solidarity. But she wants to continue.

                    YARA (CONT'D)
When they torture... when they target
hospitals and murder doctors... when they
use chlorine gas... when the world stands by
and does nothing... and they laugh, when the
world does nothing... that's what they do to
break us... it takes strength to hope... they
want to smash it... [looking up at the height
of the vault above] it takes faith to hope...
we tried to build something new, and look at
us... thrown to the wolves... I have a friend...
she calls hope 'obscene'.

TJ nods, understanding her.

                    YARA (CONT'D)
But if I stop hoping... my heart will stop
beating...

A moment between them.

FADE.

31. LOUNGE. EVENING

A Saturday night special. More locals than usual, and some specially invited Syrians from other places too. The tables are gone, and rows of seats have been laid out.

Above the stage a screen has been set up on the wall.

Everyone is listening to a haunting piece of music played by a Syrian oud musician.

By her laptop, with Laura helping, Yara projects her black and white photos onto the screen. Clear she has talent and has made a portrait of the village; some unusual shots too, others with a sense of humour, hinting at the eye of an outsider seeing life afresh. Perhaps teenagers by the bus stop dancing to music on their mobiles, older men by the betting shop, fingernail examination and delight after the session in the salon.

Two Syrian mums eating a fish supper. Other photos showing how tough life is; a woman on the step of her home, with boarded-up windows. The same woman with her friend, inside, having a cup of tea by candlelight.

The audience murmurs, giggles or whispers in recognition as the faces appear.

Molly is both embarrassed and touched by a lovely one of her by the window in the salon.

Gentle ones of Sadie with her daughter Josie, after the latter's hair was done.

Children demolishing their food in the lounge.

Laughter at a local child's face as she bites on stuffed vine leaves.

TJ, Jaffa, Margaret and other volunteers are at the back, carefully watching proceedings.

Enthusiastic applause by all as it ends.

Jamila, in her wheelchair pushed by Mohammed, a man in his fifties, and two others carrying what look like two poles, join Yara who has moved to the stage.

YARA
Jamila would like say a few words on behalf of us all.

JAMILA
[Reading from her carefully prepared text]
'We didn't choose to come here... it happened to us. We don't want to take from you. We want to contribute, make our own lives, and share with you. We are lucky to be here, and not at the bottom of the ocean like many others... [pause] We know from our own broken hearts the greatest gift on earth is peace, peace, peace... let us build peace and respect between us. We thank you.'

Jamila touches her heart, and acknowledges the applause. Mohammed steps forward and speaks with a strong accent, as best he can.

MOHAMMED
The hardest thing for us is that we might never see our land again... but you have given our children a chance to live. Shukran.

Mohammed acknowledges the reception too.

YARA
Our community has prepared a little gift for you... inspired by the miners' banners of these villages... and what the oak tree means to you.

The other two Syrians unfurl the banner between the poles. Applause from everyone as they appreciate the skill and originality of the banner, a tapestry of a mature oak with the words 'Strength, Wisdom and Resistance' in English and Arabic stretching out from the leaves.

TJ, Laura, Jaffa, and others at the back of the lounge are deeply touched.

FADE.

32. THE OLD OAK

Maggie arrives at the pub, opens up the front door and enters.

Inside, she heads to the bar, taking off her coat.

Upstairs in the flat, TJ pours himself a cup of tea.

> MAGGIE'S VOICE
> [Shouting from below] TJ!!!!! Come down here! Hurry!!!!

TJ rushes down the stairs and joins a shocked Maggie in the kitchen.

They confront chaos before them. Water cascades down the wall of the kitchen. It has brought down several ceiling panels which lie in a mess on the counter. It reveals the water tank above, and water gushing from it. Other panels sag, and look ready to drop. Water runs down the wall into the boiler, and into the fuse box and switches. The water is pooling on the kitchen floor despite a small drain gully grid which is not adequate for the amount of water.

> TJ
> Fuck! I'll turn off the mains...

MAGGIE

My God, what a mess…

TJ throws away a soggy panel that has fallen, kneels in the puddle, leans under the sink and tries his best to turn a rusty old stopcock to turn off the water at the mains. It takes him some time but he manages. Gradually the flow down the wall eases.

He grabs a torch from a drawer, jumps up on the counter, and shines the torch onto the water tank. He can see where the water has been gushing from.

TJ

Bastard… an old valve has given way…

MAGGIE

It's a total disaster TJ… I'll phone Laura and Jaffa.

Maggie steps further back in the lounge to get an overview of the damage. She's already on the phone on speaker by the time TJ joins her.

TJ just stares at the damage.

MAGGIE (CONT'D)

You have to come quick Jaffa… the whole kitchen's flooded… it's terrible…

JAFFA'S VOICE

Shit! What about the electrics? Are they okay?

MAGGIE

Don't know… let me see…

She switches on a light.

                              TJ
        No Maggie!

Too late. The lights flicker and blow. The fuse board shorts and
there are sparks and an almighty flash.

                           MAGGIE
        Oh shit! I'm sorry...

                              TJ
        Better call Tony, Maggie.

LATER: Laura and Tony are with TJ and Maggie as they
examine the mess in detail. Tony peers up at the water tank
from below.

                         TJ (CONT'D)
        Jaffa asked those Syrian lads to double check
        the valves... they must have messed up, or
        didn't understand... the water has run down
        into the fuse box...

Tony examines the fuse box.

                           LAURA
        I can't believe it... all the cupboards are
        destroyed too...

                           TONY
        [Still examining] I'm sorry TJ... they're
        done... total rewiring, big job. You can't use
        the lounge safely... no way.

                           MAGGIE
        Oh God, what about the bar? Did I screw that
        up too?

TONY

It's a separate ring main, the bar's fine. It's
not your fault Maggie... would have made
no difference. [Staring at it] The boiler...
kaput... that'll cost two grand... and look at
the floor... soaked the joists and subfloor... it's
all going to cost a fortune.

LAURA

The insurance will cover it...

Maggie looks at Laura and shakes her head. Laura and Tony are
shocked.

MAGGIE

We told them we'd cut off the lounge to the
public to reduce the premium.

LAURA

No insurance!

MAGGIE

Nobody was using it!

TONY

TJ?

They are concerned for him as TJ continues to stare at the
destruction for a few moments.

TJ

[Quietly] What are we going to tell the kids?
[As he walks out] How can I face them?

They watch him leave.

MAGGIE

He'll never sell the place now, and he hasn't
got a bean. [Increasingly upset, to Laura] I
wish you had listened to me!

33. BAR. NIGHT

Packed pub, late at night. Markedly different atmosphere.
Customers have had much more to drink. As well as the usual
suspects (Vic, Eddy, Garry, Joe and co) there are new faces and
some younger people too.

It is clear Vic, Garry, Eddy, and Micky have many more friends
and relatives with them; they have had a lot to drink. A few
tough young men are with them, in celebratory mood.

Charlie is close by having a quiet drink with his wife Mary, who
is in her wheelchair, but he's aware of what is going on elsewhere.

Vic and Garry are in particularly boisterous form, like a double
act, messing around and entertaining their crew, which includes
Micky.

Eddy downs his pint and moves to the bar to order another
round.

EDDY

[To TJ] Another round for the lads…

Vic and Garry join Eddy to give a hand with the round.

VIC

Good atmosphere tonight TJ… eh? Bouncing!

GARRY

Just like the old days…

TJ just continues to pour the pints determined not to be baited.
Joe and others become aware of the conversation.

GARRY (CONT'D)
None of the fucking missionary work next
door... peace and quiet.

Still no response from TJ.

VIC
Got to hand it to you TJ... you were right...
said it yourself... the lounge was falling to
pieces... just wasn't safe.

GARRY
Should have listened to your own advice
mate.

VOICE 1
Leave it lads... we're having a nice night.

GARRY
Just chatting... a bit of sympathy.

Joe cringes as the cruelty continues. Charlie pays attention now
too.

VIC
Maybe it wouldn't have happened if you'd
got a proper English plumber instead of those
fucking cowboys... that's what's wrong...
cheap foreign labour.

VOICE 2
Vic... give us a break.

EDDY
Just talking man...

GARRY

Heard a rumour about no insurance... is that
true?

Charlie hears the question and looks up. Still no answer.

GARRY (CONT'D)

Sometimes we just don't get round to things...
you know how it is... busy lives.

TJ's face is grey as he continues to focus in on each pint poured.

EDDY

You won't be selling this place in a hurry
now... [still no response] Not much to say for
yourself tonight eh?

TJ

How about shut the fuck up!?

Charlie listens too, as the tension rises.

VIC

Easy TJ, think before you leap... you'll need
the punters back now... [looking to Garry and
Eddy for support] We want to help out... let
bygones be bygones... Look at this tonight, a
full house! You look after us... we'll look after
you... [looking around the crowd, all white]
our Oak, our kind... [touching his heart] our
people.

TJ bites his tongue and takes refuge from the humiliation by
concentrating on the pints, and lowers his head to the task in
hand.

Charlie has heard every word, and stares at TJ.

Charlie finishes his drink and leaves with his wife, Mary.

34. TJ'S KITCHEN. NIGHT

TJ scrolls through Facebook on his computer.

SCREEN: The Old Oak. Back where it belongs. Rule Britannia!

TJ surveys the poisoned anonymous posts, taunting him.

He can see images of the Saint George's flag photoshopped to the facade of the pub, with logo 'Ragheads Out'.

PHOTO: INSIDE THE PUB: packed crowd. Vic (with fist in the air), Garry and Eddy downing a pint, celebratory faces.

A few more vicious racist posts, under false names.

Syrian Cowboys cause flood. TJ Ballantyne, Muslim lover.

Photo of a few Syrian men at a street corner 'Foreign paedos prowling our streets'.

Then one that shocks him. A picture of Marra. 'Pet Food', with inappropriate smiling emojis.

A large picture of TJ's face, superimposed on a target, with the single word 'Loser' above it.

He can hardly believe it and turns it off in disgust.

He slumps forward on his seat and holds his head in his hands.

35. STREET TO THE OLD OAK. MORNING

Tony walks towards the back door to The Old Oak. He looks around him before he rings the bell.

TJ answers the door. It looks like he's hardly slept.

> TONY
> I need to speak to you.

> TJ
> Another day Tony if you don't mind…

> TONY
> [Glancing around again] No TJ, now.

TJ beckons him in to the bar.

Tony seems hesitant.

> TJ
> Take a seat Tony.

> TONY
> Remember you coaching us at football? Speak your mind you said… it would always be private… Does that still hold TJ?

> TJ
> What's up Tony?

> TONY
> Got to get something off my chest… I can't bear it man… I couldn't sleep last night.

TJ takes a seat now too.

TONY (CONT'D)
But you have to promise... just between us.

TJ
You have my word.

Tony struggles for a moment.

TONY
Uncle Eddy and a couple of the lads came
round to our house last night after the pub
closed... they know my old man always has
a few beers stashed away... anyways, they
were all really pissed by the time I got back
from the club... I was in the kitchen getting
a snack... the door was half open... I heard
every word TJ.

Tony pauses for a moment. TJ holds his eye.

TONY (CONT'D)
Vic... you know what he's like after a drink...
getting louder and showing off to my old
man... everyone knew the plumbing in the
lounge was dodgy... Vic did a bit of building
work in his time... I heard him explain... the
water pressure goes up at night... all they had
to do was loosen the valve between the copper
pipe and the tank... as the pressure rises... it
would give, and nobody would know.

It's a shock to TJ.

TJ
Are you sure it wasn't the drink talking,
showing off?

TONY

Vic was boasting, Uncle Eddy too... thought
they were so clever and they would blame
the ragheads... that's what they said... Pissing
themselves.

TJ

Vic and your Uncle Eddy... anyone else?

Silence for a moment.

TONY

Charlie.

TJ

No... not Charlie.

TONY

Charlie forced the window... that's how they
got in.

TJ

No no... I don't believe that.

TONY

Charlie was there TJ. I heard him. He said
he was engaged in the hall... he asked you a
favour, to hold one meeting but you blanked
him... said he was humiliated. Never heard
Charlie speak like that... he wanted to teach
you a lesson... Vic did the dirty work but it
was Charlie's idea...

TJ is rocked.

TJ

Me and Charlie were in the same class at
school... we ate in each other's home... his
dad, my dad... we've had our run-ins, a few
tough ones... but not this...

TONY

[Pause] I'm sorry TJ. You can't tell anyone...
remember your promise... or they'll know it
is me.

TJ

[Almost to himself] I was at his wedding.

35. CHARLIE'S HOUSE

TJ walks along a street. He looks grey faced; he has hardly slept.

He stops at one familiar house which is clean and tidy and knocks
on the door. The house beside it is still a mess, more butts and
a single crushed-up can.

The front door opens, and Charlie appears before him.

Charlie just stares, wondering what TJ is up to. TJ looks around
him and then back at Charlie. Charlie can't read his mood.

TJ

Look at our town Charlie... all the things that
have happened to us... me, you... your dad,
mine... We're all in the same leaky boat... it
all happened long before the Syrians arrived...
you're not a stupid man... how did you
become like this?

CHARLIE

[Defensively] What are you on about?

TJ

[Almost to himself] We all look for scapegoats
when life goes to shit don't we? We never
look up... we always look down... who's on
the rung below us, and stamp on the poor
bastard's face.

TJ studies him for a moment.

TJ (CONT'D)

I want you to know... I know. Charlie, I
know.

He holds Charlie's eye for a long moment.

TJ turns away and walks off.

36. INT. THE OLD OAK, LOUNGE. DAY

Yara, Laura, Jaffa, Archie and Maggie sit in the lounge for a
meeting with TJ to discuss what they should do. A few of them
have pads on their knees and pencil at the ready. TJ is shrunken
and withdrawn.

TJ

It's the kids that got me... I went round every
single door to let them know... [pause] Linda,
'Don't worry TJ... nothing good ever lasts.'
Young Ryan, 'I knew it, I knew it.'

He looks up at them.

YARA

Mr Ballantyne...

TJ can't bear it and holds up his hand.

TJ

Please Yara... please...

There is something in his hurt and weariness that stops her.

JAFFA

We're not beaten yet.

LAURA

We'll organise a crowd funder, spread the
word... we'll get the place repaired...

ARCHIE

The unions will help, the church groups too...

LAURA

It might take time... but we'll get there.

TJ

'It might take time... but we'll get there'.
How many times have I heard that? A whole
lifetime of getting there, without ever getting
there... self delusion.

LAURA

[Gently] TJ... please...

TJ

Just an excuse. For failure. For getting
screwed... again and again... from the
strike... to this pub, to the state of this town
that's rotting... half the bloody country too!
The only thing that's 'getting there' is hate,
lies, corruption. It stinks to high heaven!
And betrayal! What happened here was no
accident!

LAURA

What are you talking about TJ?

JAFFA

Do you mean the damage... the flood?

TJ

No accident... it was a betrayal!

MAGGIE

You have to tell us...

ARCHIE

What's going on TJ?

TJ

Not the time...

LAURA

We need to know what happened... who did
it?

TJ

[Almost cracking] SHUT THE FUCK
UP! [It stuns them all] I can't deal with this
now! What matters is they close us down
for helping a few families fleeing war, and
our own hungry kids... families choosing
between heat and food, humiliated, in one
of the richest countries in the world. Jesus
Christ!

LAURA

[Gently] TJ... you haven't slept... easy...

138

                    TJ

I've been asleep for years Laura. I've just
woken up. I could see it in the kids' eyes…
just like the punters in the bar… dished up
shit for most of their lives… things done to
them… they don't shout, or complain, just
swallow it all… walking doormats.

Laura is broken-hearted for him. They sense TJ's despair.

              TJ (CONT'D)

Expect nothing. And you don't get hurt. Keep
your mouth shut… look after your own, law
of the jungle. That's what they've learned.

                   YARA

Mr Ballantyne… please believe me…

                    TJ

I'm tired of believing Yara… I'm tired of
trying to believe… I mean it, I'm done. It's
over.

He walks out in silence, as the door swings behind him.

37. THE BEACH

TJ walks through the sand dunes towards the sea.

He walks along the beach, his shoulders slumped, feeling numb.

He looks out towards the horizon and tries to evaluate his
position in relation to the village.

He continues along the beach, to the spot where he first
encountered Marra.

He stops. He stares out at the sea for a few long moments.

LAURA
[In the far distance] TJ!!!! TJ!!!!!

He can see a distant figure shouting and waving, as she comes over a dune.

She starts to run towards him. Laura.

As she gets closer he begins to walk slowly in her direction.

In the distance, they meet.

CLOSER: she gives him important news, which is not heard.

38. YARA'S HOME – EVENING

TJ and Laura (carrying dishes of food) head towards Yara's home.

They knock on the door, and wait in silence.

A male Syrian, not from the family, lets them in.

They enter the house and wait inside the door. TJ sees Yara, with her mum and female friends in the kitchen. One of them beckons Laura towards them.

The male friends stand separately in the sitting room.

Yara moves towards TJ and takes the dish from him.

TJ
I'm sorry, Yara.

Silence for a moment.

YARA
They found my father's body... at least we can
bury him and lay him to rest. [Pause] He was
a beautiful man.

I am sure he was.

TJ has no more words and bows his head.

Yara takes the dish to the kitchen and rejoins the other women. TJ sits beside the men in the sitting room.

TJ spots young Salim looking at him from the stairs that lead into the room. They hold each other's eyes for a moment. His heart breaks for the child in the sombre atmosphere.

The doorbell rings.

Bashir opens the front door.

He is stunned to see thirty or so people from the mealtimes; children and parents. Archie, Finn, Joe and the other volunteers are in the background. Linda is there in the foreground, alongside her friend Rima, arms linked, with Tommy on the other side.

BASHIR
[In Arabic] Mum, Yara... you should come.

Those inside move to the front door and some spread out beyond to the exterior, including Laura.

More and more are arriving.

Linda has a big bunch of flowers in her arms, so too does Tommy, and many of the kids and adults alongside them. Rima urges Linda to step forward.

LINDA
We didn't know what to do when we heard...
so I asked Rima... we all need flowers
sometimes, don't we?

Linda holds out the flowers to Yara. Yara goes to her, takes them and thanks her.

Fatima and others have come to the door.

LINDA (CONT'D)
We are very sorry for your dad... [to Fatima]
We are very sorry for your husband...
[looking around her] We are very sorry for
your country.

A moment's hesitation, then Rima and Tommy take flowers to Fatima's family.

TJ slips into the street. Betty and a couple of mothers place flowers beneath the window of the house. On an impulse Betty gives Fatima a hug.

TJ and Laura watch in silence, as the grief is shared by both communities.

One after another, many of the faces Yara has photographed in the village, come up to them, including Tania and the women from the salon.

More and more flowers, cards, and even a few lit candles in jars are laid out under the window, and perhaps on the window ledge too.

Nadia whispers to Yara. It prompts them both to go inside the house for a moment. Nadia returns with the framed picture of her father. She lays it on the ground among the flowers, the cards and the candles.

Yara lays her precious camera before his image as tribute too. She stares down at it for a few moments.

Many hug Fatima, who is overcome.

TJ spots Max there in the background, hovering and insecure. At last he comes forward with a single flower, and lays it down.

TJ and Laura are stunned as more and more arrive at the house.

TJ's eyes jump. He sees a figure pushing someone in a wheelchair, at the back, almost hiding; Charlie stands there solemnly, eyes to the ground, with his wife Mary sitting in the chair.

Yara moves to stand by TJ.

> YARA
> Now do you believe?

TJ stares out at the sea of faces, overcome by the wave of solidarity. He cannot speak. Up to a hundred have now arrived. Yara touches her heart.

> YARA (CONT'D)
> Shukran, TJ.

TJ nods quietly, touches his heart and looks out at his community.

> TJ
> Shukran, Yara.

FADE TO BLACK.

The music continues for several moments.

FADE IN as the music changes to the marching bands of the Gala.

39. DURHAM CITY, MINERS' GALA – PRESENT

Up close, TJ, with Yara by his side, and Laura, proudly hold the poles of The Old Oak banner which flutters gently in the breeze.

They march along with joy and pride, among familiar faces from The Old Oak, both English and Syrian.

The sound of brass bands and applause from the crowd grows

stronger; more banners, more marchers, a great procession snakes its way through the narrow streets.

From further back again; dozens of banners from the miners' lodges and other unions, and brass bands inch their way forward.

Yet more bands, more faces of young and old, applauding, cheering, laughing, a sense of strength and confidence.

The Old Oak banner is now a dot amongst the mass of humanity filling up the old city, on sloping streets packed and stretching into the distance with the cathedral beyond: a tradition of 136 years still endures.

FADE.

Ken Loach

Director

What was the gestation of *The Old Oak*?

We had made two films in the northeast, stories of people trapped in this fractured society. Inevitably both ended badly. Yet we had met so many strong, generous people there, who respond to these dark times with courage and determination. We felt we had to make a third film that reflected that, but also did not minimise the difficulties people face and what has befallen this area in the past decades. There was another, longer story to tell, if we could find it.

A starting point was the reality of the region's neglect. The old industries had gone – ship building, steel and coal mining – and little had been put in their place. Many of the pit villages, once thriving communities with great traditions of pride in their tradition of solidarity, local sports and cultural activities, were left to rot by the politicians, both Tory and Labour. We found that people expected nothing from the Tories, but Labour's failure was denounced – 'done nothing for us' – yet it was a Labour heartland, with Tony Blair and Peter Mandelson being local MPs. It had made not a jot of difference. The communities were simply abandoned. Many families had left, shops closed, as did schools, libraries, churches, most public spaces. Where there was no work, hope drained away, and alienation, frustration and despair took its place. Alarmingly, the far right made an appearance.

Councils in other, more prosperous areas, sent vulnerable, needy people, seen as 'problems', who depend on housing benefit to cover their rents, to places where accommodation was cheap. Conflicts were inevitable.

Then there was another twist. The government finally accepted refugees from the horrific war in Syria. Fewer came here than to most European countries, but they had to go somewhere. Again, it was no surprise when the northeast took more than any other region. Why? Cheap housing and an area that the national media barely notice.

Paul heard the stories of what had happened when Syrian families first arrived, and we began to think this was the story we should tell. But first it had to be understood. Two communities living side by side, both with serious problems, but one with the trauma of escaping a war of unimaginable cruelty, now grieving for those they have lost and worried sick for those left behind. They found themselves strangers in a foreign land. Can these groups live together? There will be conflicting responses. In such dark times, where is hope?

It seemed a tough question, and Paul, Rebecca and I thought we should look for an answer.

How did those initial thoughts evolve into the characters and story of *The Old Oak*?

Paul and I talked about the wider picture a lot. Then Paul suggested centring the story around a pub, to be called The Old Oak. The landlord, TJ, would embody the struggle, with a history of being active in the community but now beset with problems. Stories are about relationships, and Paul then wrote of a Syrian woman who learned English in refugee camps working with international volunteers and taught herself to be a photographer. These experiences widen her perspective on the world around her. Her friendship with TJ is the core of the story.

How did you ground the characters who are living in the village, those who reject newcomers?

As always, we listened and learned. After years following social conflicts and struggles, we know what to expect, but the precise way events unfold and people react is always revealing. What became clear is that in everyone's position there is a truth. The problem is, what do people learn from their truths? You wait a long time to see a doctor – who is to blame? School classes are too crowded, who is responsible?

There are no immediate villains here. A sense of grievance can drive people to extreme measures, but there is always a logic to how they behave. To miss that is to cheapen the drama.

This village is part of a wider community. It has a long history of standing up to exploitation and attacks, first by the older mine owners and more recently by Margaret Thatcher and the enforced closure of the pits. These struggles taught solidarity and the value of international support. But the weakening of union power left individuals to fend for themselves. Look after number one, 'there is no such thing as society', the worship of the entrepreneur, these are shifts in consciousness that may overwhelm the old values. And affect whether the Syrian families are made welcome or not. And so we listened, observed, and Paul wrote the script.

How did you want to portray the Syrian families who arrive in the village?

The principle is always the same. Listen, observe and allow the people to be true to themselves. Casting is critical. It was clear that Syrians in the film should be those who have settled in the area. Paul's script allowed them the freedom to contribute so that the story was a true reflection of their experiences.

The details were important, and we all learned a lot. As in all groups, people are different. Some families were traditional, some less so. Some had learned English; some had found it difficult – I sympathised with that. All were generous with their time, many committed wholeheartedly to the project, and the cakes they brought to the set became legendary!

We were lucky to find two people who guided us through our developing relationship with the Syrian families. Yasmeen Ghrawi was invaluable during the casting and from time to time during the shoot. Sham Ziad became our link to the families, sensitive to all the questions that arose day by day.

Sometimes we had to slightly amend the details as we went along. Some Syrian mothers did not feel comfortable being seen to enter a pub and were concerned that their heads should remain covered. There was always an answer and it was important that everyone felt respected and at ease. We had a lot of laughs and made many friends.

And the rest of the casting?

After the script, casting is the most important element of any film. In *The Old Oak*, we wanted everyone apart from the Syrians to come from the local community. All the different responses to the Syrians' presence came from people who lived in the same streets, shared the same history and knew there had been good times before the bad ones. Then it becomes apparent that the same experience can be interpreted in contrasting ways, the conflicts of the drama spring from the same source.

It followed that we should find people who seemed part of the very landscape of the village. No one assumed an accent that was not theirs. They could drop into one of the real pubs and be taken for a local. This might seem a limitation, but it was the opposite. We found so many talented people, from established actors to relative newcomers and those whose lived experience made an immediate impression.

Kahleen Crawford has been our casting director for many films and she, Carla and Eliza worked hard to ensure that we met everyone who might fit the bill. After so many films I should not be surprised at the ability of so many to make fictional situations seem real. Everyone we met had something to offer, and we were left regretting that an already large cast was not even larger.

Apart from TJ, Yara and Charlie, who we mention below, there were many critical roles to cast. Two of the hardest were Vic and Garry, who take a strong line on the arrival of the Syrians. Chris McGlade and Jordan Louis understood what drove that hostility. They committed to present that without apology or overplaying the scenes. It is important for the story that the audience understands Vic and Garry, that they are credible. I felt that Chris and Jordan achieved this without compromise – a real achievement.

Two other key roles were Laura, one of the few in the village who welcome the newcomers from the start, and Fatima, the mother of Yara and three younger children. Clare Rodgerson's positivity, warmth and optimism were vital ingredients to the story. Meet Clare and you cannot fail to be struck by her energy and clear understanding of the real tensions in the region, similar to those in the film.

Amna, who played Fatima, like all the Syrian mothers, was eager to express her gratitude for being given a home and for the kindness of strangers. The stories of war, cruelty, torture and loss were devastating, and we marvelled at the strength of the human spirit that enables people to retain their humanity. Amna had the essential quality of credibility. She made the fiction seem real.

It was to Amna that I turned if there was a difficult question about how to make scene work. Maybe there were cultural details where I needed guidance. Amna's help was invaluable.

Who is TJ?
TJ is a man in his late fifties, born and bred in the village. He began work in the pit just before the strike in 1984. The experience made him a militant and he became a leader in the community, organising football for the local youngsters.

When the pit closed, he did various jobs. When his father lost his life, his mother was able to buy a pub with the compensation, The Old Oak. The village thrived and so did the pub. Later, when TJ inherited it, the pit had closed, without work the local economy collapsed and TJ has done his best to keep The Old Oak open. It is the last pub in the village.

But TJ is struggling. His marriage failed, his one son lives a distance away, he gives up his community activities and keeping The Old Oak going becomes his sole concern. He understands only too well the politics and social consequences of what has happened but has lost the will to fight back. Like so many, he knows who is responsible for the hardship he sees and experiences and knows also they have been betrayed by those who profess to speak for them. He has one reliable friend, his little dog, Marra. She asks for nothing and is always there to make him smile.

Then the Syrians arrive. A new set of demands and now he's on the spot. The film is, in part, the story of how he responds to this challenge. He doesn't have an easy choice; moments of personal despair weaken what's left of his optimism. He meets Yara and is touched by her and the Syrians and the story they tell, but does he have the strength to intervene on their behalf in this small, divided community?

Working with Dave Turner was a real pleasure. He knew the story in his bones. He has run a pub. But, more importantly he lived the story truthfully as we filmed it day by day. We could not imagine anyone else as TJ.

Who is Yara?
Yara is the eldest of Fatima's children, in her early twenties. After escaping the war, they lived in a refugee camp, probably in Lebanon. It was a transformative experience for Yara. The international volunteers took her under their wing, she learned languages, particularly English, worked alongside organisers, teachers and medics, and understood how to communicate with people from every kind of background. It meant that she became more cosmopolitan in her outlook, which probably led to issues with her mother, now happily resolved.

Yara's father is a major presence in her world. He's a tailor, a good craftsman, a thoughtful man and caring father. He has spotted Yara's talent and does his best for her, as for all his children. He and Yara's mother are close – it is, was, a secure family. Then her father crosses the authorities, and he is now in prison in Syria.

Yara is quick to read their present situation. They are placed in this village in England, on the northeast coast, where the beach is polluted by industrial waste and the first encounter with local people is hostile. It is natural that Yara, speaking the language, is the first to make contact but it takes guts and the confidence of youth to walk into a crowd of strangers. But she does it. And TJ can't help but be impressed by her courage. It is the beginning of a friendship. Whether it can be sustained is another matter.

Finding someone to play Yara led us to see people here and from Syria. Film directors, friends from the region, made good suggestions, we saw many people on Zoom, and three came to Newcastle. They were all brilliant, but of course, different. Ebla was the closest to the character Paul had written. Like Dave Turner and TJ, Ebla became Yara from day one. Her simple, direct way of communicating, linked to a personal warmth and empathy, meant that she became an integral part of the team immediately. Sometimes Ebla would not know the camera had found her, but I knew that her eyes were always bright with concentration, and her commitment would be as intense as ever.

Who is Charlie?
Charlie is a good man. A boyhood friend of TJ, they grew up together, families close, and their adult lives have been similar. Whereas TJ was active in the community, Charlie was a quieter, family man, probably a couple of kids, one of whom, a daughter, lives nearby.

He and his wife Mary bought the terraced house they had rented when it was offered at a reasonable price. They have always seen it as both a secure investment and their permanent home. But they have had bad luck. Mary has a long-term illness which confines her to a wheelchair. Other families have left, houses have become cheaper, new neighbours take over the streets, some bring problems, and the community of good neighbours is no more. Charlie and Mary are stuck. The imagined serene, secure retirement will not happen.

Charlie, like so many, feels let down. The Old Oak is his regular haunt, where he can have a quiet pint with friends, and that helps him look after Mary, and the two of them take pride in their well-kept house and their supportive kids. But it is a tenuous hold on what is left of his hopes. If there is one more unexpected problem for him and Mary, Charlie might crack. Even as a good man, there is only so much he can take.

Trevor Fox, who plays Charlie, was the quiet stalwart in the team. Trevor is not only a fine actor of great experience, he is also from the area, lives there and is embedded in the daily lives of the characters Paul describes. He understood the unspoken disappointment of Charlie's life and his deep need to hang on to what is familiar and reassuring. The other side of Charlie is that he too remembers the solidarity of the miners during the strike, the principles they stood by, and how those strengths seem increasingly irrelevant in today's world, where individualism triumphs over the collective. Charlie wouldn't put it like that, but he'd feel it just the same. Despair can drive us to extreme action. Trevor captured that, a crucial element in the story.

The film is set in 2016 and you don't specify which northeast village we are in. Why?

2016 was the year the first refugees from Syria arrived. Clearly there had been insufficient preparation, as it was 2016 that the story that triggered Paul's interest had happened. A bus carrying refugees was met with hostility, and it took a lot of hard work to establish good relations.

When we prepared and shot the film, Durham County Council were extremely helpful, and Syrian families appreciated their welcome. There were still tales of random acts of aggression, but gradually they are fading. But decisions by central government stir trouble. Why place refugees in deprived areas where people have very little, where the social infrastructure is already under pressure, and the general neglect is so long established it is not a news story anymore? Well, simply by putting the question like that, we know the answer.

The village in the film is not a single village in real life. We knew Easington already, some of us had worked there and we had friends there. Paul had made the sea an important part of the story, and although the beach at Easington is no longer black with sea coal, it is still marked by industrial waste. Neighbouring Horden has a visually impressive collection of terraced streets, a classic example of traditional miners' houses, built to gather round the pit. And Murton had an empty pub, a lovely building, with a friendly owner who helped us enormously. But while these villages were good places to work, they are typical of many, and this story could be set in all of them.

To summarise, making three films in the northeast has been a powerful experience. The clichés are true – a warm and generous people, a stunning landscape, and a culture built on hardship, struggle and solidarity. While the details change, that is also true of so many working-class areas where we have been lucky enough to work: Glasgow and Clydeside, Liverpool and its rival Manchester, South Yorkshire and beyond. These were not chosen at random; they are the regions where writers have written their stories. There are other areas, of course, with equal claim to the same qualities – hardship, struggle and solidarity. The last of these is our strength. One day we have to be so organised, so determined, that our collective solidarity will end the hardship and the need for struggle. We have waited long enough.

Rebecca O'Brien
Producer

What's the background to *The Old Oak*?
Having done *I, Daniel Blake* and *Sorry We Missed You* there was a feeling that there was another story to tell in the northeast. It was partly that the stories Paul [Laverty] was picking up while he was researching those other two films were forming in his head – he felt that was another level of story to tell.

We would have done it a couple of years ago: Paul was ready to do more research and get writing, but then the pandemic hit and that stymied us. The research is very detailed, and it takes months and months not just for Paul, but for Ken [Loach] who goes around with him. They met many people from the ex-mining community in County Durham and people like Dave Turner, who plays TJ, showed them around (and it was always in the back of their minds that he might be in the film).

Then Paul came up with the idea of having a pub and having a look at the communities from the local point of view; having a look at the situation where refugees have been placed in these relatively poor areas, which have been undervalued since the main industry left. We ended up with a feeling that it would be good to tell that story from the point of view of the local community.

When did you start to see *The Old Oak* as the third part of a trilogy?
I think Ken felt that there's a symmetry – or an asymmetry – in the idea of having three stories set in a similar milieu. We'd had such good experiences working on both *IDB* and *Sorry We Missed You* that it seemed like this would be the area to tell the story

in. And there is something balanced about a third one. It wasn't intended to be a trilogy but I suppose people will call it that.

Once you had a script what did you do next?
Once I've got the script, I will then go and start sending it to our usual supporters. In this case, it made total sense to go to the people who supported us on *I, Daniel Blake* and *Sorry We Missed You* and see if they would come on board. In truth it was nerve-racking post-pandemic as to whether they were going to do it. Our French partners Why Not the production company and Wild Bunch the sales company have been incredibly supportive over the last 15 years so I didn't doubt that they would back us. We do also need to have that British endorsement and so we also went back to BBC Films who were supportive on the other two, and they said yes, absolutely. Then I approached the BFI to see if they would help fund this film, as well as StudioCanal to make a trio of British funding. And then we're in a co-production with our regular Belgian partners Les Films du Fleuve. As before, we're spending money in Belgium and bringing Belgian technicians over to work with us which we love. But with Brexit that does mean that visas have come into the fray, as well as carnets, which means it's been more difficult to do a European co-production. Luckily our partners have stuck with us and just said, 'No, we're not bothered about that. We'll just keep doing it.' So though it involves more administration, it's been possible.

How was the casting process?
Casting took a long time, more than normal because it's a bigger cast but also because we wanted to cast a young woman who was Syrian and during the pandemic it was very difficult to do that. We have two particular filmmaker friends in the Middle East who were helpful and sent us a list of actresses that they thought would be of interest to us. And indeed they were. We cast Ebla Mari as Yara, who just shone. Having cast her, normally it would take three weeks maximum to turn it round and get

her visa. In this instance we didn't know how long it was going to take because there were no more priority visas because of the Ukrainian situation – and the Home Office was being completely unhelpful in telling you where you were in the list. Luckily, because she'd already just had a visa to come over to be auditioned they couldn't very well deny her coming over and being in the film. It just meant that we had to push the film for two weeks because we had no guarantee we were going to get her in. That costs money but it was worth the push.

Also, it was important to us that the Syrian families were authentic. The people in the film who play the Syrians are Syrian families and refugees who came here four or five years ago and made their homes here. Some of the situations in the film are very familiar to them: things that they have experienced.

How did this film compare in the making to the two previous northeast pieces?
It's a much more complex film, because normally in our films we're dealing with maybe one community. Here, we have two communities. We had to represent the local families and the local pub goers, and then within the pub group, you've got people who are in favour of the refugees being here, and you've got people who are against. It's a complex tapestry of characters and people and families. The Syrians needed extra support in terms of explanation, what they're expected to do, how we pay them… all those elements are quite complicated. And with that bigger cast there are quite a few big scenes with lots of people, showing both communities celebrating, or both in sadness. It's a complex structure. I mean, it would have been much easier for us to have done this one before *I, Daniel Blake* and *Sorry We Missed You*!

If *I, Daniel Blake* and *Sorry We Missed You* were broadly tragic, is *The Old Oak* an attempt to end the trilogy on a more positive note?

There is no easy answer. People do their best in difficult circumstances, not of their making. We have tried to unravel a few knots, share the experiences of people trapped by war and social conflict. We hope audiences will see their situation a little more clearly now. Who knows?

Cast

Dave Turner
Ebla Mari
Claire Rodgerson
Trevor Fox

Dave Turner
TJ Ballantyne

How did you come to be cast?

It's a very long story but briefly, before I retired from the fire service in 2014, I was a full-time union official. When Sixteen Films came up to the northeast to make *I, Daniel Blake*, they sent out some enquiries to local trade unions and a friend of a friend put me forward. I was totally naive. I didn't even realise what I was going for – I literally walked into a Newcastle labour club and bumped into Ken Loach. I had a chat with him and then I was called back three or four times, but I never knew I was auditioning, genuinely. He gave me a lovely part in *I, Daniel Blake*, but it was a small part. Then when they came back up to the northeast to make *Sorry We Missed You* they got in touch, and they gave me a small part in that, a lovely role. Then it all went quiet for a little while, although Paul [Laverty] kept in touch with me.

It was probably early 2019 when he said, 'Would you like to meet for a coffee?' We had a bit of a chat, talking about the pub where I was working at the time and the problems in County Durham with the pit villages where they've just been left to rot. I took Paul for a drive around some of the villages and he saw how bad it is – that was around February 2019. He came to the pub where I worked and spent quite a few hours because it was full of characters. The pub was actually called The Oak Tree. I think it was in June 2019 that I got a phone call saying would you be interested in driving Ken Loach around for a few hours? Would I! That's really a hardship! So I drove Paul and Ken around a lot of the villages and you could see they had something in their minds. Then COVID came but Paul and Ken did keep in touch.

Last year (2021) it was obvious that there was something in the offing regarding a film and I was asked to go in. I did a lot of auditions, and they were much more difficult, more serious, more difficult subjects: domestic violence, racism, substance abuse. I realised that I wasn't going to be getting the jokey part. And then the last time I auditioned was in December and I think I did seven scenes in an afternoon. Most of them were with people who've got parts in the film funnily enough, but I remember walking out of the County Hotel in Newcastle just being absolutely drained. I walked across to the pub and had to have a pint just to collect my thoughts. The week before Christmas Ken rang me and said, 'I would like to offer you the part.'

I didn't realise until a few weeks later that it was *the* part. And from then it's just been a matter of trying to get my head around it.

You don't get a full script at the beginning. What did you know about TJ and his backstory when you started filming?
I knew his name; I knew he owned a pub that had been left to him by his late mother. I knew his father had died. I knew his marriage had broken up – I wasn't living with my wife and child anymore. I was in a pub that was in a village and the pub was on the bones of its arse. That was basically it.

Who is TJ? What's his story?
He's a good man. Ex-miner, his father was killed in a mining accident and as a consequence of that his mother bought The Old Oak pub. She's been dead 20-odd years and he wanted to help his mother, but his marriage has broken up, he's living in the poverty zone and the pub is struggling – as are most of the village pubs around. It's the only public space left in the village. Because of what's happened to TJ, he's lost. He had been an organiser in the village – previously he ran football teams;

everyone knew TJ. But because of what's happened to him he's just been beaten down and he's withdrawn into himself. Then one day, some Syrian families move into the village. And that's where the story of TJ in this film starts.

What's TJ's response to the arrival of the Syrian families?
The way I played it was he didn't want to be involved. He didn't want to go back to being active and he couldn't be bothered. I identify with that – I was a trade union official and by the time I was retired I was just worn out. When you get to a certain age and you've been doing something for so long, and then somebody comes along who's 30 years younger and they're full of enthusiasm you look back, and you just think, 'Well, that was me, but I can't be arsed now.' That's the way I've played TJ: he's washed up, he's had enough. But then he develops these relationships with two women – Ebla [Mari], who plays Yara and is an amazing young woman and Laura, played by Claire [Rodgerson], who I auditioned with a couple of times last year and I love to bits. And these two young women have given him the kick up the pants he needs. He starts to do what he can. But then, just as he's coming out of his down period, he has a couple of huge personal setbacks, through no fault of his own. And then he's back at the bottom, where he was previously.

TJ's best friend is his beloved dog, Marra. How did you get along with Lola, the real Marra?
I did over 1,000 miles to get to know the dog, because it was a 50-mile round trip every time I came to see her. I started in February, coming down once or twice a week, every week. It was just due to the generosity of the owners of the dog, Steve and Michelle, who welcomed me into the house and said, 'Have a cup of coffee and then you can take Lola for a walk.' I did it for four months. It created an ease – she would just walk alongside me without a lead, respond to the name 'Marra' and she was lovely.

How close do you feel to TJ?

The problem I've had is I've taken it on. I've become TJ and that's something I've had to get my head around. I'll be honest with you, the first day was not that difficult, because it was just me with the dog, and it was just filming on the beach. Then the second full day's filming was a scene in the pub with a lot of the actors. I found it incredibly difficult. In the first two weeks I had a massive case of impostor syndrome. You're sitting talking to people who have been acting for years and years. And they're bloody good. And I've walked in off the street and I've got the lead part in a Ken Loach film. I now realise there was a hell of a lot of guilt. I felt I shouldn't be here. It took us the first three weeks to get over that. It's taken a toll on us physically and emotionally and I would never have believed that possible. But as I say, I've never been in this position before. I started to enjoy it once Ken said to us, 'It's not easy to enjoy it at the time but you will look back on it with enjoyment.' And he was right.

Ebla Mari
Yara

How did you come to be cast in *The Old Oak*?
Last November (2021) a Palestinian director called Annemarie
Jacir contacted me and said that she was helping the production
here to find a Syrian actress. She knew an actor from the village
I'm from, Majdal Shams in the occupied Golan Heights, which
is a Syrian place occupied by Israel in 1967. I gave her a video
from a play I was doing and then had a meeting with Ken
[Loach] and casting director Kahleen Crawford on Zoom. It
was only 15 minutes but we chatted about where I'm from, a
general chat. Then I auditioned on Zoom and I was so bad! And
then I came and auditioned in real life in March (2022). It was
improvisation only, some in Arabic, some Arabic/English, some
only English – they didn't say anything about the character or
the story. I only knew that the character is a photographer and a
refugee. Four days later Ken called me and asked me if I would
like to be in the film.

What were you told about Yara in the first instance?
Not a lot! But I knew her situation because I went to visit
Syrian refugee families here in the UK. But that's it. I know
what's happened in Syria. I know the horrible, horrible stories
that happened and are still happening. I was against the regime.
But I also watched a lot of documentaries in preparation for
this role about the revolution in Syria and what happened after
that, what's happening to Syrian detainees and what they are
experiencing there. I researched where Yara came from and what
happened to her. I researched the refugee camps – but not who is
Yara. Because maybe Ken wanted me to be myself but different.

Is what people see in the film an accurate portrayal of what some Syrian families have gone through?

Yes of course. Ken and Paul and Rebecca and the production, you can feel the effort that they want to portray the right narrative. They asked a lot of the Syrians here in a meeting to speak about their personal experience. Most of them were detainees in Syrian prisons and were tortured for doing nothing. After hearing their stories Ken told them that he knows how serious this should be for them. But in the story of the film, they are not focusing on what happened in Syria. This is a story of two communities.

Who is Yara?

She's a refugee who came here with her family. She doesn't know where her father is because he was taken to prison and that was the last she heard of him. And I know real people who still don't know anything about their fathers, where they are. Nothing. So my father, Yara's father, he gave me a camera because I love to take photographs. This is the only thing I have from him and it is very emotional for me because he believed in me, believed that I want to be a photographer. After fleeing the war my family lived in a refugee camp in Zaatari in Jordan – imagine that. We went there to a hostile, hard place, not because the people are bad, but because they are victims too, because of what's happening to them. They have nothing and their life is hard. So we came here, and we are all victims. Yara faces a lot of hostility but then she meets TJ and they form a friendship. Yara wants to make life here easier and more friendly and to forge a friendship between the two communities. That's very similar to what TJ's role is, building bridges. You feel empathy towards Yara because she faces a lot of racism. You will see it.

What is Yara like?

I feel like she's brave. She stands up for herself. She's also sociable. And sometimes I'm not like that, I'm not as sociable as she is.

I stand up for myself, but I feel she's stronger than me, which I like - I feel that sometimes I learn from her bravery and her social confidence, in terms of going out there and trying to make a point or trying to fulfil something good. I wouldn't be as active as her. She's not apologetic about that. She believes in what she thinks. The rules don't come from above and she has to obey them. I mean she's respectful, but she's her own person, which I like. She's more of a modern woman, so she decided not to wear the hijab. In the refugee camp she was a volunteer and she met a lot of people from around the world. She saw lots of different versions of life that she could relate to, that she wanted to experience or to discover.

What does photography mean to Yara?
Firstly it's something she loves, but also, because her father gave her a camera, it's a way to see life through both her eyes and her father's. She's trying to see hope through the ugliness and unfairness of the world. The camera gives her hope. Ken and I talked about hope – she's trying to see the good and the beautiful moments and to capture them as a way of searching for hope. Also, taking pictures is a way of resistance for her. She's waiting for her father to come back so she can show him her best pictures. Photography for her means three things: a way of documenting, resistance and hope. Those three things are important to me too.

How did you learn to be a photographer?
I spent two days with Joss [Barratt, photographer] going around and taking pictures of people. He taught me how to hold the camera and support it and find the light. That bit isn't hard, but taking the right pictures, beautiful pictures, is hard. I studied theatre and I love visuals: my dream is to be a filmmaker. So I think I can see what's beautiful. But to capture something real, to notice things that other people walk on by, to really see... that is difficult.

Claire Rodgerson
Laura

Who is Laura?
Laura is an old family friend of TJ's. They used to be activists together, probably doing anti-austerity stuff. Then TJ has kind of lost his way but Laura has kept on fighting for the community while trying to build a family and hold down a job. When the Syrian families arrive she wants to be a positive force to bring the communities together.

What is her background?
'An irreverent force of nature' is how she was described in the script! She doesn't take any shit but just believes that the community can be better. She's a fighter. And she hasn't given up like TJ. That's what I'm like in real life – you can't just give up and accept the fate that's been dealt to you by the powers that be. I'm from round here, I'm from Sunderland. I guess Laura and a lot of people like her – and like me – are sick of only ever lamenting the past. And no one ever talking to us, or trying to support us to build a future and just slowly strangling these communities – someone's got to fight that. In Laura's particular case, her mam was active in the strike, running the kitchens and whatnot, so when you're from a political, activist family, there's a kind of osmosis that happens as well. That's where she gets her drive from.

How did you come to be cast in *The Old Oak*?
I work for a national charity called Citizens UK and we have 17 local chapters, one of which is Tyne and Wear Citizens. I'm an organiser within that chapter. We have orbited around Ken

[Loach] and Paul [Laverty] making these films in the northeast for a while – when *Sorry We Missed You* had a premiere, for example, we ran a campaigning workshop after it so that people didn't go out thinking we're powerless and we're all doomed. Somehow, I ended up meeting Paul [Laverty] when he was doing the research for the film. He came to Sunderland, met a few people who are involved in our work and was introduced to me, because part of my background since moving back to the northeast has been working with young people who have been drawn into the politics of the far right. We had a nice chat, and I just got on with my life. Then, when they were casting this film someone came through my trade union looking to speak to women who are active in the community. I thought, 'Alright, I'll just go and meet Ken Loach, that'll be quite nice.' The first time I'd acted in my whole life was doing that improv for the first audition. Then they kept asking me to come back and eventually they said we'd like to offer you this part.

How much does the story of *The Old Oak* speak to your working life and experience?

There are elements of the film that I have seen in my life. I've seen the racism. I've seen the people fighting the racism. I've seen people believing that we're stronger if we act together rather than fighting over arbitrary divides that the ruling classes have determined for us. I've seen all of that. The northeast in particular is a really segregated place. There are pockets of integration and moments of beauty but I had not lived in the northeast for a long time and I still can't get over how segregated it is. There's this idea from the Blair age of 'problem communities'. It's not problem communities, it's problem systems, problem scapegoating and problem dumping.

Part of the story of *The Old Oak* is how often these issues are ignored...

Yeah, exactly. I think that's why I'm involved in this project. So we can tell this story. If this was just some love story or something it wouldn't be for me. I'm in this film because it shows resilience, that we can fight, we don't have to roll over to the fate that's been determined for us by politicians who don't give a shit. Nigel Farage paraded down this very bit of coastline a few years ago saying that he gave a shit about working-class people in the northeast. Fuck him. This is the opposite of that story. People are really trying in these communities. And to be able to tell that story is an absolute honour, and to be able to tell a story of immigrants and people who aren't white standing shoulder to shoulder to try and make things better is really important to me. You're stronger when you act together, and you might not be that different after all. That's my work in the northeast and my reason for being here.

Trevor Fox
Charlie

Who is Charlie?

Charlie's a guy who lives in the village and drinks in The Old Oak. He's a very old friend of TJ [Dave Turner] the landlord; they've been through a lot together. They went to school together, their dads worked in the pit together. TJ made a speech at his wedding and they go back years and years. Charlie's wife Mary is disabled and they have a daughter. They own their own house, they're very proud of the fact that they come from the village but things have got really rough for them. All the housing around them is getting sold off and what once was like a thriving, nice place to live has become a nightmare. And he can't get out: their house is now worth like a quarter of what they paid for it. So they're just fucked. They're stuck there, there's nothing he can do and he feels totally helpless.

What does Charlie want?

The village to be back the way it was. But that's not going to happen so he wants to get out. He'd like to be able to sell the house and move somewhere nice. They wanted to move up to be next to where his wife's sister lives, they thought about doing it a while ago, but that's impossible now because they're just stuck in their house with a mortgage. He's living a total nightmare. The next-door neighbour is a lunatic, frightening his wife, there's rubbish all over the streets. It's just a living hell.

What does The Old Oak mean to Charlie?

The pub's the last place he's got in the village where he can just kind of go and forget about his troubles. At one time there was

the Miners' Welfare, there were community centres, but that's all gone now. All they've got is the pub. You can go there and you can forget about things for a little while. I mean, he doesn't drown himself in alcohol. He's not an alcoholic, or anything like that. He can just meet with the lads, have a crack, just have a couple of hours out of the misery that is more or less the rest of his life.

What is Charlie's reaction when the Syrians arrive?
Charlie's reaction is that he's not against immigration. He's not against refugees. But why is it always their village or villages like theirs that get them? You see him say during the course of it that they never put them in London next to all the posh people, they put them next door to us and we've got nothing. And what little we've got we've got to share out with other people. It's just another group of people who have been placed in the village who won't be supported properly and the people in the village will have to pick up the pieces. Well, they can't anymore. It's gone too far now.

What is Charlie's predicament?
He really doesn't know what to do but he feels like he's got to do something. So he makes the wrong decisions. In life that happens to us, doesn't it?

How did you come to be cast?
I first auditioned for Ken Loach in 1988 for a film called *Riff Raff*. I've met him several times since over the years, and I did some voiceovers for him on the documentary about the welfare state [*The Spirit of '45*]. And then I came in and met him again for *I, Daniel Blake*. I've met him several times over the years, but it's just never worked out, but I mean obviously, it's Ken Loach – I've always wanted to work with him. And then just on this one, I was actually doing a job in London and they were auditioning in Newcastle. So even though I live in Newcastle I had to come

home from the job in London. I met him, and then it came down to a few auditions, I improvised with Dave [Turner, TJ] and with a few of the other lads who were in the pub, and then after three or four auditions they said, 'Yeah, we'd like you to do it.' I mean I think that the reason Ken cast me is because he didn't want George Clooney to do it. He saw something in me that was close to Charlie.

What's your connection with the northeast?
I come from a town called Wallsend which is an ex-shipbuilding and coalmining town. The pit shut when I was a kid, and then the shipyards closed when I was at school. My background as an actor is I've done a lot of work in community and political theatre. I've toured all these towns, done shows here, performed in community centres, worked in the Miners' Welfare. My extended family, this is where they live, in outlying towns around Newcastle, in ex-pit villages. It's in the family. It's in the blood. It's in my DNA.

Crew

Fergus Clegg
Joss Barratt
Sham Ziad

Fergus Clegg
Production Designer

What design challenges did the script for *The Old Oak* present?

The big thing was finding the pub. It was clear in the script that the pub was a character as much as any other. And so it was finding something that looked right, had the architectural interest of an older building and contained echoes of its former glory in the architecture. Most pubs have that tradition of being the centre of local life in their city or town or village. We wanted to get that feeling of some backstory to the building. You wanted a sense of previous owners, because in each pub you go to there's a sort of accretion of development that takes place over time. It starts off as one thing and develops as fashions change. And so you go in and you see all the different layers of a pub, from its original features to those that have been changed in the 70s or 80s.

The script also called out for a room at the pub where you could hold the functions, one that was big enough to hold 50 people. That was unusual. There's a slight element of the working men's club, or miners' colliery club there.

You always hear pubs are closing five every week, or whatever it is, so we thought we'd be awash with options. But it turned out we weren't. Because we were too late: they've already been redeveloped. We'd found that there were a lot of pubs that had 'gone missing' in the intervening years since the end of mining. With the closing down of the mines, the revenue stream in the villages had gone.

But we found a pub in Murton with a room at the back that if we did some building work, we could modify it enough to make it just about big enough for what we had in mind.

How did you work up the interior of The Old Oak?
The function room is supposed to have been mothballed for 20+ years so we had to decide on a look for that room that was different to the rest of the pub. The look of it is more 60s – metal furniture, formica tables and things. The rest of the pub is still in the world of a traditional pub with woodgrain, wainscot detailing on the walls, traditional wallpaper and nicotine stains. But for the function room there were a lot of very good photographs taken by Keith Patterson in Easington of the very same situation in pubs and in soup kitchens that were set up in rooms to feed the striking miners and their families. So that was a good reference. We also had to build a kitchen because that's part of the story.

Was the function room actually functional?
Yes. That's the thing with Ken [Loach] – everything has to work. It was a proper building site. We were making the beer run properly so we could use the pumps, and we had the kitchen set up so it would function as a kitchen.

How did you find other locations and houses for the film?
Part of our backstory is that you can come up here and buy a house for £6000 so we thought, 'This is going to be straightforward.' But the ownership issues are complex. There are some landlords who are decent and others who are less so; some are housing associations, some are council owned. Some are tenanted and the tenants have got issues around drug use, or mental health, or both. We homed in on a few that were cooperative and responded. There's a lot of offshore ownership, people who don't want to be known, don't want to be involved. So we alighted on Tea Street in Horden for Yara's house. There were houses on that street that were cooperative. Ken has a particular dislike of white UPVC doors and windows – they're very bright and contrasting with red brick and that on film for Ken is very invasive. He doesn't like red, white or bright colours in general so one of my

big job is toning down the palette. And of course many houses have exactly that. The quick way of doing it was with adhesive vinyl. We found a muddy grey colour that Ken liked and had a team of sign installers just going round to these allocated areas and covering over the UPVC windows with this vinyl.

How did you make sure the Syrian houses were portrayed authentically?
To start with we spoke to people who were involved in housing refugees and then we spoke to several families, one of which we got very friendly with – they would invite us around for fantastic meals. We went around to four or five homes early on and asked them for their experience from their flight to their arrival here. In the beginning the local councils were very badly prepared but as things progressed they had houses that were decorated, furnished to a degree, but only with the absolute minimum. We'd start the house with that kind of look – generic British furniture sourced by the council with some food packages sourced by charities. We asked the families what they'd try to get first and it was always proper utensils for cooking – because traditional food helped to preserve their identity. We would feel the same. They had brought some items that they put on the walls, reminders of home. Throughout we were led by the Syrians. We learned a lot and we were all moved by their enthusiasm and willingness to help.

Joss Barratt
Photographer

What part does photography play in *The Old Oak*?

Photography is the thread that stitches the locations and the characters and all the narrative together. It's the device that links Yara to her history, to her present, and to her exploration of a new place and a new people. It gives her the licence to look and see. And then photography is also the device of how we self-select. It reflects what we choose to see and what we choose to remember. Because what we don't see, we then start to fill in with our imagination. So photography in the film is the prompt to what has happened, what is happening, but also what isn't there.

What does photography mean to Yara [Ebla Mari] in the film?

She was always going to be a photographer. I don't think she's a professional photographer but it's always been part of her makeup. And the camera is then the gift from her father, which becomes the icon of how she expresses herself. Even more so in a foreign land. Because when you go anywhere, as a photographer, what you see first off is your big, first impression.

What coaching did you give Ebla?

Joss's photography school was not remotely technical: it was making sure she had the right camera that would be accurate to her age and circumstance and where she'd come from. So she has a very good camera, but a 10-year-old very good camera with a not very expensive lens, but one that does everything. That was a choice. In order to get Ebla into thinking like a photographer, we just spent a few days walking the streets in Newcastle. My tutoring was not technical, more about approach and intention. If you approach someone with humour, and with engagement, then that's 90% of what they'll give back to you. That starts before you've even left your room in the morning. It's like, 'What am I going out to see? What am I going to look for? What's my motivation for taking any of these pictures? What am I trying to show?' Photography, when it really works, is this fantastic, dual-facing prism: it shows who you're photographing and who you are simultaneously.

There are two sets of stills montages that feature in the film. How did you capture them?

The conceit is that all the photography we see in the film is Yara's photography. For the title sequence Yara arrives at this rather hostile reception committee. Her pictures that we see were meant to be instinctive, reactive, sort of jaggedy, compositionally uncomfortable snapshots of what she saw when her family arrived in the village.

Later Yara exhibits a photo essay, a slideshow, to the community in order to show them what she's been doing with that camera. At least three of them are Ebla's actual pictures. The idea was to get her competent enough to take some of them – every time you see her on screen with her camera she was shooting live pictures. Some of those ended up in the final slideshow. What I was trying to elicit from her is not how to do it but *why* you're doing it – what it is to be a photographer and what it is to make those connections with people.

Sham Ziad
Syrian Cast Coordinator

What was your role on *The Old Oak*?

I was Syrian cast coordinator, translating sometimes, informing the Syrian families what time they had to come the next day, what they had to wear, everything, basically. When they arrived I welcomed them, took them to their costume, checked they were alright and asked them for their opinion about the scene.

How did you become involved in the production?

I am a Syrian refugee myself. I came here seven years ago and I've been involved in projects like translating for Syrian families before. In November last year (2021) Gateshead Council called me and asked me if I'd be interested to meet Ken.

How much of the Syrian families' experience do you recognise?

In my case, I didn't experience any racism, but people around me did. It's there, I can't deny it. A lot of my input has been to do with Syrian culture back home. Or Syrian names or accents – we have so many accents back home. People from different cities speak different dialects. I wanted to make sure that everything would look and sound right. I wasn't involved in casting the Syrian families but they gave me their information and I contacted them to learn about them.

How did you come to the UK?

I left Syria in 2012 and went to Egypt because my house in Damascus was bombed. My dad said it is not safe anymore, so we went to Egypt. We declared ourselves as refugees hoping they

would take us to another country. We waited for four years to get to any country in Europe and then they called us in 2016 and said are you ready to travel? We said yes, please, because we know that Egypt is not safe for Syrian families either. In January 2017 we travelled to the UK. I was excited. It's safe, I can finally be stable in a house, not having to move around all the time.

When you saw in the film refugee families being bussed into communities in the northeast what did you think?
It happened to me. You feel like you're lost. You don't know how to start. You have to remove all your past life and start again, new language, understand a new culture. For example, you can go and talk to the police here. Back home you can't. You can talk to teachers at school or uni here. Back home you have to talk to them in a really formal way. These are small details but we're not used to this environment.

What did you make of the northeast when you arrived?
To be honest it was depressing. I came here when I was 26 and didn't know where to start. I couldn't integrate, I didn't have a social life or friends here. Now I'm studying a Masters in International Relations, Conflict and Security. Basically, when I got to Gateshead the council took care of me. They provided refugees with a social worker to look for jobs and for me, when they found out my English was okay, they told me how to get more English skills that would take me on to studying at uni.

What do you think of the story told in *The Old Oak*?
It's amazing, it's really touching, and I think everyone will really love it. The film shows the pain that Syrian families must go through. It's not easy to move your life from one country to another. We didn't have a choice. We were forced to leave home.

A Brief Note From Paul Laverty

At the outset there are endless possibilities before diving in to write a screenplay. A screenplay cannot be copied from the street, but it can inspire. Getting lost, wandering, watching and listening are greatly underestimated. I am particularly indebted to all the Syrian families who shared their lives with us. Many did not want to be named in case it would endanger their families back home. Activists too could not have been more generous, again too many to list. But I must thank Sara Bryson who suggested many great notions, and through her I had the great luck to cross paths with John Barron, Val Barron and their network of volunteers who organised to welcome Syrians and had the insight and dedication to organise games and food to local youngsters during their summer holidays. Solidarity in action. I would like to pay a special thanks to Sham Ziad and Yasmeen Ghrawi for their advice, friendship and encouragement, always a source of inspiration.

I had the great fortune to become friends with the remarkable historian Howard Zinn for the last 10 years of his life. I thought of his quote as we finished the shoot. Thank you Howard and RIP.

> 'To be hopeful in bad times is not just foolishly romantic, it is based on the fact that human history is a history not only of cruelty, but also of compassion, sacrifice, courage and kindness.
>
> What we choose to emphasise in this complex history will determine our lives. If we see only the worst, it destroys our capacity to do something...
>
> And if we do act, in however small a way, we don't have to wait for some grand utopian future. The future is an infinite succession of presents, and to live now as we think human beings should live, in defiance of all that is bad around us, is itself a marvellous victory.'